More than **Trivia**

Interesting Stories and Fascinating Facts

B. Craig Jones

More than Trivia
Interesting Stories and Fascinating Facts

Copyright © 2023 by B. Craig Jones

ISBN: 978-1-955664-03-5 (PB)
ISBN: 978-1-955664-04-2 (HB)

Library of Congress Control Number: 2023943452

No part of this publication may be reproduced, stored, or transmitted in any form or by any means without the prior written permission of the copyright owner except for a review for insertion in a magazine, newspaper, broadcast, website, blog, or other outlet.

Trademarks mentioned are the property of their respective owners. The author or publisher endorses no product, brand name, or trademark mentioned here, nor is the material in this book endorsed or approved by any person or organization.

This book is a compilation of material that comprises a collective work. The original expression of material, its arrangement, and the collective work is copyrighted by B. Craig Jones. The material is meant to inform and entertain. It does not give medical, financial, life, or other advice. Always seek competent professional advice for your situation.

The author used due diligence to verify the information provided. However, if information becomes out-of-date or if there are inaccuracies, the author and publisher accept no responsibility for them and specifically disclaim any liability, loss, or risk, personal, professional, or otherwise, which may be incurred as a consequence, directly or indirectly, of the use and/or application of any of the contents of this book.

Doozybird
Publishing

www.doozybird.com
Sherwood, AR

Contact info:
craig@doozybird.com

Table of Contents

Introduction	1
People	3
Inventions	23
Human Interest	37
Music	47
Sports	61
Places	71
Food	89
Movies & TV	109
Celebrations	117
Curiosities	125
Companies	145
Fun & Games	153
Culture, Customs, & Laws	157
History & Language	169
Health & Medical	181
Science & Engineering	185
Travel & Transportation	193
Tech	199
Plants & Animals	205
Geography	221
Weather & Astronomy	225
Other books by B. Craig Jones	233

Introduction

If you are fascinated by interesting stories, as I am, then you picked up the right book. And the great thing about these stories is that they are all true. There are also a few short facts here that you may find in other trivia books, but only a few. Instead of having hundreds of mere trivia facts, I have included only a handful and selected just the particularly interesting ones. The focus here is on the slightly longer stories about people, places, and more. In the stories here, you get interesting details but not so many details that it becomes tedious to read. After reading some of these stories, you may find yourself sharing some of them with family and friends or on social media. All-in-all, there are 777 facts and stories in 21 categories that are uniquely interesting. The stories average about 76 words each, making them easy to read anytime and anywhere. So, take a minute or ten minutes and read and enjoy yourself. You deserve it!

I am truly grateful that you selected my book, and I hope you get a lot of enjoyment from it. If you are so inclined, please leave a review on Amazon. That really does help me out.

B. Craig Jones

Chapter 1

People

#001 William Patrick Hitler, half-nephew of Adolf Hitler, emigrated to the United States and joined the U.S. Navy in 1944, fighting against his half-uncle and earning a bronze star.

#002 Sean Connery started bodybuilding at 18 before becoming an actor and entered the Mr. Universe bodybuilding contest in the early 1950s. His website says he placed third in the 1950 competition.

#003 Robert LeRoy Parker was the actual name of outlaw Butch Cassidy. He was the eldest of 13 children from a Mormon family. He got his famous nickname because he served a brief apprenticeship as a butcher (Butch), and he had a cattle thief friend whose last name was Cassidy. His death at the hands of the Bolivian Army in 1908 is in dispute. Family members and those who knew him have said that he escaped death in South America, returned to the United States, and lived out his days in the Pacific Northwest until he died in Washington State in 1937. Some say he had visited his hometown of Circleville, Utah, several times before his death and is buried near there.

Interesting Stories and Fascinating Facts   **More** than **Trivia**

People

#004 Herb Cobb McDonald introduced the all-you-can-eat restaurant style in Las Vegas in 1946. The original midnight chuckwagon buffet cost $1.25 and later became the 24-hour Buckaroo Buffet for $1. McDonald was a big promoter for Las Vegas and was considered a godfather of publicity and marketing. He brought the Beatles to Las Vegas in 1964, where 17,000 fans paid $2 to $5 to see them. His father was a fishing buddy of baseball legend Ty Cobb, the source of Herb's middle name.

#005 Alvin "Junior" Samples, a 6th-grade dropout, was a carpenter by trade, a race car driver, and a fisherman. He went on a radio show when he was 40 and told a humorous story about catching the biggest fish ever seen in his hometown. The story became a best-selling novelty record called *World's Biggest Whopper*, which led to him getting invited to join the TV show *Hee Haw* when he was 43. He stayed with *Hee Haw* until his death 14 years later. He and his wife Grace had five children.

#006 Geraldine "Jerrie" Mock always thought that girl activities were boring and, at age 7, announced that she wanted to be an airplane pilot. At 19, she dropped out of college to marry and had three kids. But the dream of flying still stirred within her, and at age 38, she became the first woman to fly solo around the world. Her 22,850+ mile trip started in Columbus, Ohio, in March 1964, lasted 29 1/2 days, and had 21 stopovers. Flying eastward, one of her early stopovers was in Saudi Arabia, where she caused quite a stir when they discovered there was not a man on board. Women were not allowed to drive a car in Saudi Arabia, much less a plane, until over 50 years later. Instead of landing at the Cairo Airport in Egypt, she mistakenly landed at a secret military base. Today her plane, the *Spirit of Columbus*, hangs in the National Air and Space Museum of the Smithsonian.

More than Trivia   *Interesting Stories and Fascinating Facts*

People

#007 Johnny Weissmuller, winner of five Olympic gold medals for swimming, was also an actor. He played Tarzan in twelve movies in the 1930s and 1940s and is well known for the "Tarzan Yell." The sound is a registered trademark and service mark owned by Edgar Rice Burroughs, Inc., a company founded by the author of the Tarzan books.

#008 Nigel Richards (born 1967) is considered the greatest Scrabble tournament player ever. He won the 2015 French World Scrabble Championship despite not speaking French (he spent nine weeks memorizing the French dictionary). He is a five-time World Champion, five-time U.S. national champion, eight-time UK Open champion, and a 15-time winner of the world's biggest Scrabble competition, the King's Cup in Bangkok.

#009 William Frederick "Buffalo Bill" Cody was considered the most recognizable celebrity in the world by some historians in 1900. In 1883, he established Buffalo Bill's Wild West Show, an outdoor entertainment that showcased the western frontier. The show featured shooting displays, historical reenactments, cowboy performances, wild animals, and more. The show toured Europe eight times, with audiences including Queen Victoria and other European royalties. Buffalo Bill's London tour concluded in 1887 with over 300 performances and 2.5 million tickets sold. The Wild West Shows employed 1,200 performers and many animals. Buffalo Bill later co-founded Cody, Wyoming, and owned eight thousand acres of land there. He built the Irma Hotel, named after his daughter, which is still operational today. Buffalo Bill has been portrayed in numerous films and TV shows, honored with two U.S. postal stamps, and several landmarks named after him. Additionally, the Buffalo Bills NFL team was named after him.

Interesting Stories and Fascinating Facts **More** than Trivia

People

#010   Calvin Cordozar Broadus Jr. is the birth name of the actor and rapper known as "Snoop Dog." His parents called him Snoopy because they thought he resembled Charlie Brown's dog Snoopy, and he also liked the character.

#011   Fred Baur was a chemist that invented and received a patent for the Pringles potato chip container and packaging method. He was cremated when he died, and some of his ashes were placed in a Pringles container at his request. There were several flavors to choose the container from, and for Baur, of course, they chose the Original flavor.

#012   Several well-known people do not go by their birth names for one reason or another. Here are some examples: Kareem Abdul-Jabbar (Ferdinand Lewis Alcindor Jr.), Alan Alda (Alphonso Joseph D'Abruzzo), Woody Allen (Allan Stewart Konigsberg), Michael Caine (Maurice Joseph Micklewhite), Patsy Cline (Virginia Patterson Hensley), Kirk Douglas (Issur Danielovitch), Bob Dylan (Robert Allen Zimmerman), Carmen Electra (Tara Leigh Patrick), Elton John (Reginald Kenneth Dwight), Eminem (Marshall Mathers III), Gerald Ford (Leslie Lynch King Jr.), Jamie Foxx (Eric Marlon Bishop), Lady Gaga (Stefani Joanne Angelina Germanotta), Judy Garland (Frances Ethel Gumm), Cary Grant (Archibald Alec Leach), Ice Cube (O'Shea Jackson), Hedy Lamarr (Hedwig Eva Maria Kiesler), Michael Landon (Eugene Maurice Orowitz), Marilyn Monroe (Norma Jeane Mortenson), George Orwell (Eric Arthur Blair), Annie Oakley (Phoebe Ann Moses), Jack Palance (Volodymyr Palahniuk), Pink (Alecia Beth Moore), Jane Seymour (Joyce Penelope Wilhelmina Frankenberg), Charlie Sheen (Carlos Irwin Estevez), Shania Twain (Eilleen Regina Edwards), Conway Twitty (Harold Lloyd Jenkins), Vin Diesel (Mark Sinclair), John Wayne (Marion Robert Morrison), Whoopi Goldberg (Caryn Elaine Johnson), Stevie Wonder (Stevland Hardaway Judkins).

More than Trivia   *Interesting Stories and Fascinating Facts*

People

#013 Marion Donovan invented a waterproof diaper cover that was sold at Saks Fifth Avenue in 1949. Two years later, she sold her company and the diaper patent for $1,000,000. She had 20 patents in her lifetime, typically practical solutions to home problems.

#014 The *Crocodile Hunter* TV personality and Australian wildlife expert Steve Irwin has a snail named the *Crikey steveirwini* after him. "Crikey" was a favorite expression of Irwin's. The rare snail species are found in tropical rainforests at altitudes over 3,000 feet. Its shell color resembles the Crocodile Hunter's favorite outfit – khaki.

#015 Abraham Lincoln was fond of cats and sometimes brought home a stray one. When he was elected president, he was given two kittens that he named Tabby and Dixie. He once fed Tabby from the table during a White House formal dinner, much to the embarrassment of his wife, who said that was "shameful in front of their guests." He replied, "If the gold fork was good enough for (former President) Buchanan, I think it is good enough for Tabby."

#016 23-year-old female runner Bobbi Gibb hid in the bushes at the starting position of the 1966 Boston Marathon, waiting to sneak into the 26-mile race. She previously applied for the race but was turned down. The race director wrote her back, saying that "women were not physiologically capable of running marathon distances." But Gibb had been training for this race for two years, sometimes running 40 miles daily. She jumped into the race after about half the runners had gone by. She was soon discovered, word spread, and people were cheering her on. The governor of Massachusetts was at the finish line to shake her hand, and she finished ahead of two-thirds of the runners. There is a statue in Hopkinton, Massachusetts, honoring Gibb called "The Girl Who Ran."

Interesting Stories and Fascinating Facts   **More** than **Trivia**

People

#017 Princess Elizabeth turned 18 during World War II. At that time, she joined the women's branch of the British Army and trained as a truck driver and mechanic. She was the only female member of the royal family to join the armed forces.

#018 Early French artist Francois Clouet (1510-1572) used crayons for his elaborate modeled portraits. They so impressed Henry V that he was knighted and became a court painter for royalty.

#019 Genghis Khan was unique in his management style in that he emphasized performance, talent, and effort rather than wealth, social class, or who you know. In fact, some of his former enemies became his most trusted generals because of their skills and experience. This system or style is called meritocracy and dates back over 2,000 years.

#020 Joshua Slocum was the first person to sail solo around the world. His voyage of over 46,000 miles took him three years. Adventurer, seaman, shipbuilder, and writer of an international best-selling book, he never learned to swim, calling it useless. Slocum's vessel for his historic voyage was a gift from a friend who said it "wants some repairs." It was a rotting oyster sailboat named *Spray* that was propped up in a meadow away from the water. Slocum spent $553 (equivalent to ~$17,000 today) and 13 months for the repairs. In 1899 he wrote about his voyage in his book, *Sailing Alone Around the World*. He later bought a small farm in Martha's Vineyard but could not adapt to life away from the sea, so he sailed and spent winters in the Caribbean. He was making plans in 1909 for a new South American adventure. However, on one of his winter voyages, he disappeared at sea and was never heard from again.

People

#021 Wayne Allwine was a voice actor who was the official voice of Mickey Mouse for 32 years. In 1991, he married Russi Taylor, the official voice of Minnie Mouse for 33 years. She also voiced Pebbles Flintstone in *The Flintstone Comedy Show* in 1980 and many other characters.

#022 Calvin Cordozar Broadus Jr. (aka Snoop Dogg) released a cookbook in 2018 titled *From Crook to Cook: Platinum Recipes from Tha Boss Dogg's Kitchen*. It has a foreword by Martha Stewart and was on Amazon's bestseller list in 2022 after his Super Bowl and Puppy Bowl appearances.

#023 Author J.K. Rowling is truly a rags-to-riches story. Her first manuscript, *Harry Potter and the Philosopher's Stone* was rejected by 12 publishers before Bloomsbury Publishing bought it in 1997. Her books have gone on to sell over 600 million copies and have been translated into 84 languages. Her fortune has been estimated at over $1 billion.

#024 6' 6" Kevin Joseph Aloysius "Chuck" Conners played Major League Baseball (1949 and 1951) and professional basketball (Boston Celtics 1946-48) before starting his 40-year (1952-1992) TV and movie career. Before his sports career, he was a tank-warfare instructor for the Army during World War II. He was chosen from over 40 other actors to play the part of rancher Lucas McCain on *The Rifleman* TV show. He initially turned it down because he could earn more as a freelance actor. But a few days later, the producers saw and were impressed by his performance in *Old Yeller*. They offered him more money for *The Rifleman* and a 5% ownership of the show, which he accepted. *The Rifleman* was Soviet leader Leonid Brezhnev's favorite show, and the two men later became friends. *The Rifleman* was one of the few American TV shows broadcast in the Soviet Union at the time.

Interesting Stories and Fascinating Facts　　**More** than **Trivia**

People

#025 Teddy Roosevelt's oldest child, Alice, had a pet garter snake named Emily Spinach. She kept it in her pocketbook and would take it out at the most unexpected times. Alice was 17 years old when her father became president. He remarked, "I can either manage Alice or the country, and I can't do both."

#026 Ada Lovelace, born in 1815 and daughter of English poet Lord Byron, is often called the first computer programmer. She was trained in mathematics early on and was introduced to Charles Babbage (born 1791), the "Father of the Computer" when she was 17. Babbage showed her the prototype for his mechanical computer called the difference engine. Babbage was impressed by her intellect and analytic skills and called her "The Enchantress of Number." Lovelace saw the potential of Babbage's Analytical Engine, going beyond being a mere number-crunching machine, and she published the first algorithm to be carried out by such a machine.

#027 Augusta and Adeline Van Buren, sisters descended from Martin Van Buren, the eighth president of the United States, became the second and third women to drive motorcycles across the United States. They set out to prove that women could ride as well as men and would be able to serve as military dispatch riders. They rode Indian PowerPlus motorcycles equipped with gas headlights and dressed in military-style leggings and leather riding breeches. During the ride, they were arrested numerous times, not for speeding but for wearing men's clothes. Despite succeeding in their cross-country journey, the sisters' applications to be military dispatch riders were rejected. Adeline continued her career as an educator and earned her law degree from New York University. Augusta became a pilot and joined Amelia Earhart's Ninety-Nines international women's flying organization.

More than Trivia *Interesting Stories and Fascinating Facts*

People

#028 Bert and Ernie on *Sesame Street* got their name from Bert, the cop, and Ernie, the taxi driver in Frank Capra's movie *It's a Wonderful Life*.

#029 Marie Curie won the Nobel Prize for Physics in 1903 at the age of 36 and for Chemistry in 1911. She was the first woman to win a Nobel Prize, the only woman to win it twice, and the only person to win it in two scientific fields.

#030 William Phelps Eno (1858-1945), known as the "Father of traffic safety," created several innovations in road safety, including the stop sign, pedestrian crosswalk, one-way street, and traffic circle. Yet, he never learned to drive a car.

#031 Mary Wollstonecraft Shelley was visiting with some writer friends in Geneva when she was 18 years old. One of the writers, Lord Byron, suggested a contest to pass the time to see who could write the best scary story. Mary won the competition with her story, *Frankenstein*, published anonymously two years later. Her real name first appeared in the second edition, published in Paris three years after the first edition.

#032 An Italian bank manager named Gilberto Baschiera collected approximately $1 million from affluent clients over seven years. However, he didn't take the money for his own use. Instead, he transferred it to less privileged clients so that they could meet the criteria for loans. Some of these clients managed to return the money as Baschiera requested, but others could not, and eventually, he was caught in 2016. Although he was a first-time offender, he received a two-year prison sentence. However, he did not serve any time after a plea bargain, and this modern-day Robin Hood lost his job and home.

People

#033 Michael Kevin Kearney was a child prodigy from the U.S., born in 1984. At age six, he finished high school in one year. By age 10, he had a Bachelor's degree in anthropology and, at 14, a Master's degree in chemistry. He later earned a Master's degree in computer science at age 18 and won over $1 million on game shows.

#034 The real name of the stand-up comedian known as "Larry the Cable Guy" is Daniel Lawrence Whitney. He was born in Nebraska and credits his college roommates from Texas and Georgia for helping him perfect his Southern accent impressions. From 2000 to 2006, he was part of the Blue Collar Comedy Tour alongside Bill Engvall and Jeff Foxworthy.

#035 Heron of Alexandria, a Greek mathematician and engineer born in 10 AD, was one of the earliest Foley artists (someone who creates sound effects for the entertainment industry). He made many innovations for the Greek theater, including a device that mimicked the sound of thunder using the mechanically timed dropping of metal balls onto a hidden drum.

#036 Painter Bob Ross, the host of *The Joy of Painting*, developed his interest in art after attending an art class at the military base in Alaska where he was stationed. After spending 20 years in the Air Force, mainly in Alaska, he retired as a Master Sergeant in 1981. Before retiring, he earned more money from painting than his military salary. Ross painted in a 16th-century oil painting style widely called wet-on-wet, which enabled him to create a painting in 30 minutes. Ross painted an estimated 30,000 paintings in his lifetime, typically landscapes with mountains, snow, lakes, or log cabins inspired by his time in Alaska. The TV show, *The Joy of Painting*, ran from 1983 to 1994.

More than Trivia   *Interesting Stories and Fascinating Facts*

People

#037 After Williamina Stevens' husband abandoned her and her son in her early 20s, she found employment as a maid for Edward Charles Pickering, the director of the Harvard College Observatory (HCO). Her skills beyond that of a maid were noticed, and Pickering invited her to join the HCO. During her career, she discovered several nebulae and stars, and she made the first discovery of a white dwarf star. She was the first American woman honorary member of the Royal Astronomical Society of London.

#038 Our nation's 7th president, Andrew Jackson, was a tough character. Jackson joined the Continental Army at 12 and fought in multiple sword fights. Once, he fought a gun duel where his opponent shot first, hitting Jackson in the chest. The wound was not life-threatening, and he fired back, killing his opponent. At age 67, while leaving the U.S. Capitol, a man aimed a pistol at Jackson, which misfired. The man pulled out a second pistol, which also misfired. Jackson, in turn, sprung into action beating the man back with his cane until others came to his aid.

#039 Abebe Bikila, a marathon runner from Ethiopia, won his first gold medal in the 1960 Summer Olympics in Rome while running barefoot. He bought new running shoes in Rome, but they gave him blisters, so he ran barefoot. He won the race beating the world record by eight-tenths of a second. He was hospitalized with acute appendicitis almost six weeks before the 1964 Tokyo Olympics and had an appendectomy on Sep. 16. He entered the Olympic marathon on October 21 and won the race finishing over 4 minutes ahead of the second-place finisher. When he died in 1973 from complications of an auto accident four years earlier, his state funeral was attended by 65,000 people, including the Emperor of Ethiopia.

Interesting Stories and Fascinating Facts   ***More* than Trivia**

People

#040 When President Andrew Jackson, aka "Old Hickory," died, his pet parrot, Poll, was at the funeral. Apparently, Poll had picked up some choice cuss words along the way. Some say that Poll got excited because of the crowd, but for whatever reason, Poll let loose with a string of loud cuss words and had to be removed from the premises.

#041 Edmund Thomas Clint was a remarkably talented child from India who created an impressive collection of over 25,000 paintings during his short life, despite passing away from kidney failure just before his 7th birthday. His artwork has been showcased in numerous exhibitions across India. At the tender age of 5, Clint even won first place in a painting competition for artists under 18.

#042 King Croesus of Lydia (585 BC - 546 BC) was renowned due to his immense wealth. He is also recognized for introducing the first gold coins. His father, Alyattes, also developed coin minting using a combined gold and silver alloy called electrum. The plentiful reserves of electrum in the Pactolus River, located in Sardis, the capital of Lydia, were associated with the legend of King Midas.

#043 *Star Trek* TV series creator Gene Roddenberry was a war veteran who flew 89 combat missions in the Army Air Force during World War II and later worked as a commercial pilot. After he died in 1991 at 70, some of his ashes were flown into space on the Space Shuttle *Columbia*, with more of his ashes launched into an Earth orbit on a satellite in 1997. Unfortunately, the satellite fell out of orbit in 2002 and disintegrated into the atmosphere. In recognition of his contributions, Roddenberry was honored with the first-ever star on the Hollywood Walk of Fame for a TV writer in 1985.

More than Trivia *Interesting Stories and Fascinating Facts*

People 15

#044 In 1992, President Abraham Lincoln was honored as an "Outstanding American" by the National Wrestling Hall of Fame. At 6 feet 4 inches tall, Lincoln had around 300 wrestling contests and only one defeat in twelve years.

#045 R. L. Stine is an American novelist called the "Stephen King of children's literature." Books include *Goosebumps*, *Fear Street*, and many more. He was also the co-creator and head writer for the Nickelodeon children's television series *Eureeka's Castle*. He started writing at 9 when he found a typewriter in his attic and began to type stories and joke books. He has sold over 400 million books.

#046 Jewish scientist Albert Einstein had the opportunity to be Israel's second president after the 1952 death of Chaim Weizmann, their first president. Weizmann stated that Einstein was "the greatest Jew alive" and wished him to be his successor. Prime Minister David Ben-Gurion extended the invitation to Einstein, joking to an assistant, "I've had to offer the post to him because it's impossible not to. But if he accepts, we are in trouble." Einstein declined the invitation because of his age, inexperience, and personal shortcomings for the position.

#047 Genghis Khan, one of the most formidable and brutal conquerors of all time, established one of the first international postal systems, called the Yam, over 1,000 years ago. As he controlled over 11 million square miles of land, he needed to stay informed of military and political events and keep in touch with his network of spies and scouts. This early version of the Pony Express was a well-organized series of way stations that allowed riders to travel as much as 200 miles a day with goods and information. The speed of this vast communication network was unprecedented for that period.

Interesting Stories and Fascinating Facts **More** than **Trivia**

People

#048 James Leprino, the founder of Leprino Foods, is the leading mozzarella cheese manufacturer worldwide. His company produces 85% of the cheese used in pizzas across the United States, including popular chains like Domino's, Pizza Hut, Papa John's, and Little Caesars. Leprino started the company in 1958 with just $615 after his father's grocery store, where he worked, closed. He focused on producing cheese for pizza, and that decision has paid off. He's now ranked as the 265th richest person in the U.S., with a net worth of $3.1 billion.

#049 Chuck Norris, born Carlos Ray Norris, was named after his father's minister, Carlos Berry. He was not athletic in his early years and was shy and average in school. Norris joined the Air Force in 1958 and was sent to Osan Air Base, South Korea, where he developed an interest and started training in martial arts. He has multiple black belts, including a 10th-degree black belt in American Tang Soo Do and an 8th-degree black belt in Taekwondo. During the time he competed, Norris met Bruce Lee, and they became friends. Later he joined Lee in the 1972 movie, *The Way of the Dragon*.

#050 Shizo Kanakuri was a Japanese marathon runner who dropped out halfway through the 1912 race at the Stockholm Olympics due to illness. A local family nursed him back to health. Embarrassed by his "failure," he quietly returned home to Japan without notifying race officials. He subsequently competed in the 1920 and 1924 Summer Olympics and is honored as the "father of marathon" in Japan. In 1967, Swedish Television contacted Kanakuri and offered him the opportunity to finish the race he had started almost 55 years earlier. He accepted and finished the race at age 75 with a total time of 54 years, 8 months, 6 days, 5 hours, 32 minutes and 20 seconds. He commented, "It was a long trip. Along the way, I got married, had six children and 10 grandchildren."

More than Trivia *Interesting Stories and Fascinating Facts*

People

#051 Frankenstein, the mythical creature in Mary Shelley's book, was a vegetarian, as was Shelley. Frankenstein said, "My food is not that of man; I do not destroy the lamb and the kid, to glut my appetite; acorns and berries afford me sufficient nourishment."

#052 Ingahild Grathmer is a pseudonym for Queen Margrethe II of Denmark, an accomplished painter. She sent some illustrations to J. R. R. Tolkien, which impressed him and were used for Danish editions of *The Lord of the Rings*. Margrethe's drawings were redrawn by the British artist Eric Fraser for the Folio Society's English edition of *The Lord of the Rings*, first published in 1977. Another skill she possesses is costume designing, having designed the costumes for the Royal Danish Ballet's production of *A Folk Tale* and the 2009 Peter Flinth film, *De vilde svaner* (The Wild Swans). She also designs her own clothes and is known for her colorful and sometimes eccentric clothing choices.

#053 Colonel Harland David Sanders had a wide variety of jobs before he sold his first Kentucky Fried Chicken (KFC) franchise when he was 62. His father died in 1895 when Harland was five. His mother had to work away from home, so Harlan had to cook and look after his siblings. At age 10, he got a job as a farmhand, and he left home at 13. Along the way, he worked as a streetcar conductor, a blacksmith's helper, a fireman, a lawyer, insurance salesman and started a ferry boat company. He had some setbacks and had to move back in with his mother. In 1930 he ran a service station in North Corbin, Kentucky, and opened a restaurant and motel there. He had other setbacks but continued to develop his "secret recipe" and his patented cooking method for his fried chicken. After franchising, the company grew quickly, and Sanders sold it for $2 million in 1964 at 73 and lived to be 90 years old.

Interesting Stories and Fascinating Facts   **More** than **Trivia**

People

#054 Martial arts master Bruce Lee could do 1,500 push-ups with both hands, 400 with one hand, 200 with two fingers, and 100 with one thumb.

#055 Marie Antoinette used a nail file-like tool made of pumice stone carved into a pencil-like shape to trim and shape the edges of her nails.

#056 Alphonse Bertillon, a French police officer, is credited with creating the standard "mug shot" – a photograph of an arrested or jailed person taken by law enforcement. While photos of prisoners were taken as early as the 1840s, Bertillon developed a complete and consistent process in 1888. This involved capturing the subject's full face and profile views using standardized lighting and angles. Despite some considering Bertillon as highly eccentric, he made significant contributions to the study of forensics. Interestingly, he is mentioned in the Sherlock Holmes story, *The Hound of the Baskervilles*, where a client of Holmes refers to Holmes as the "second highest expert in Europe" after Bertillon.

#057 Before Wally Amos became well known for his Famous Amos Chocolate Chip cookies, he worked as a mailroom clerk for the William Morris Agency. He later became a talent agent there, signing Simon & Garfunkle and heading up the agency's rock 'n' roll department. He sent potential clients some of his homemade chocolate chip cookies. He represented musicians such as Marvin Gaye, Diana Ross, The Temptations, and Sam Cooke. In 1975, he opened a cookie store in Hollywood with the help of a $25,000 loan from Marvin Gaye and Helen Reddy. In 1982, company revenues were $12 million. Sales declined after that, and he later sold the company. A few years later, Amos created a new cookie brand called "Chip and Cookie," after two characters he created in the 1980s.

More than Trivia *Interesting Stories and Fascinating Facts*

People

#058 Fred Gwynne, the 6' 5" tall actor who played Herman Munster in *The Munsters* TV sitcom, was a talented vocalist, painter, writer, and illustrator of children's books, including *A Chocolate Moose for Dinner* and *The King Who Rained*, both available on Amazon.

#059 Sarah Josepha Hale strongly advocated for a national Thanksgiving holiday for 17 years, writing to five presidents. She was also an early supporter of women's higher education and helped found Vassar College in New York. She founded the Seaman's Aid Society in 1833 and raised funds to build the Bunker Hill Monument in Massachusetts. She wrote over 50 books and numerous poems, including "Mary Had a Little Lamb." In 1837, she became editor of *Godey's Lady's Book* (formerly *American Ladies' Magazine*) and held the position for 40 years. Starting with 10,000 subscribers, the magazine grew to 150,000 by the time she retired at 89. Hale and *Godey's Lady's Book* were major influencers on women's and American life during that period.

#060 Steve Jobs, the co-founder of Apple Computer, visited a Sony facility in Japan in the 1980s and saw the employees wearing uniforms. Jobs liked the idea and thought Apple employees wearing identical Apple vests would help promote a team attitude. That idea did not go over well. However, in this process, Jobs became friends with the Japanese fashion designer that made the uniforms for Sony, Issey Miyake. Jobs still liked the idea of a personal uniform or brand, so he asked Miyake to make him some of the black turtlenecks he was so fond of. The designer made and sent him hundreds, enough to last him the rest of his life. Interestingly enough, in 1986, one year after Jobs left Apple (he returned 12 years later), the company did launch a clothing line called The Apple Collection. It was a big flop.

Interesting Stories and Fascinating Facts **More** than **Trivia**

People

#061 Mel Blanc, known as "The Man of a Thousand Voices," was a highly influential figure in the voice acting industry. He performed the voices of numerous iconic cartoon characters, including Tweety Bird, Yosemite Sam, Bugs Bunny, Daffy Duck, Porky Pig, Sylvester the Cat, Pepe Le Pew, Speedy Gonzales, Elmer Fudd, Foghorn Leghorn, Tasmanian Devil, Marvin the Martian, Barney Rubble, Dino, and many more. At the top of Blanc's gravestone is Porky Pig's famous phrase, "That's All Folks."

#062 William Pitt, Walter Willis, and James McCartney are some names you may not recognize because they go by their middle names (Brad, Bruce, and Paul, respectively). Other "middle namers" are Henry Beatty (Warren), Troyal Brooks (Garth), Hannah & Mary Fanning (Dakota & Elle), Audrey Hill (Faith), Geethali Jones (Norah), Joseph Kipling (Rudyard), Christopher Kutcher (Ashton), David Heyworth Law (Jude), Samuel McGraw (Tim), and George Welles (Orson).

#063 Thor Pedersen, 44, left his home in Denmark in October 2013, intending to visit all 203 countries in the world without flying. He figured it would take him four years, but like many things in life, it took longer. After riding in container ships, boats, trains, buses, taxis, and rickshaws, he returned home in late July 2023 – almost ten years later. But like Earl Nightingale said, "Never give up on a dream just because of the time it will take to accomplish it. The time will pass anyway." When Pedersen left, his motto was, "A stranger is a friend you've never met before." Despite many setbacks, he could not remember a country where he did not experience kindness or support from the people he met. Now he can point at any of the 203 countries in the world on a map or globe and say, "I've been there."

More than **Trivia**   *Interesting Stories and Fascinating Facts*

People

#064 Shortly after leaving office, our first president, George Washington, built one of the largest distilleries of that day in 1799.

#065 Button Gwinnett is not a well-known name, but he was one of the 56 signers of the Declaration of Independence. Because of the rarity of his signature, his autograph is among the most highly sought by collectors.

#066 At 7 feet 11 inches tall, Canadian woman Anna Swan Bates was one of the tallest women ever. By her 15th birthday, she was 7 feet tall. In 1863, at age 17, she started working with showman P.T. Barnum. While visiting a circus in Nova Scotia, she met and later married 7 foot 9 inches tall Martin Van Buren Bates, known as the "Kentucky Giant." When they retired, they built a home in Seville, Ohio, with fourteen-foot ceilings and eight-foot tall doors.

#067 Fred McFeely Rogers, aka Mr. Rogers, had a difficult childhood. He had frequent bouts of asthma, was shy and overweight, and was bullied and called "Fat Freddy." He overcame his shyness in high school and became student council president. He earned a Bachelor of Music degree and a Bachelor of Divinity and was an ordained minister of the United Presbyterian Church. His TV show, *Mr. Rogers' Neighborhood*, began in 1968 and ran through 2000, airing 895 episodes. The show emphasized young children's social and emotional needs. A red knit cardigan sweater Mr. Rogers wore on the show is on display at the Smithsonian Institution in the National Museum of American History.

Interesting Stories and Fascinating Facts **More** than **Trivia**

Chapter 2

Inventions

#068   ATM PINs were initially intended to have six digits. When the inventor tested the system on his wife, she could only remember four digits, which became the world standard.

#069   Inventor Levi Hutchins of Concord, New Hampshire, created the first American alarm clock in 1787. Since he made it to wake himself up for his job, it only rang at 4 AM and was not adjustable, and he never patented his invention.

#070   Play-Doh was not originally a product for children. It was created by soap manufacturer Kutol Products for Kroger in the 1930s to clean coal residue from wallpaper. The company struggled during the 1950s as the market changed and the demand for wallpaper cleaning putty decreased dramatically. Nursery school teacher Kay Zufall, sister-in-law to one of Kutol's employees, read how the wallpaper cleaner could be used for modeling projects. She let some of her students play with it, and they loved it. She encouraged the company to market it to children and even came up with the name Play-Doh.

Inventions

#071 In 1993, at the age of 8, Abbey Fleck invented the Makin' Bacon microwavable cooking plate. This product was endorsed by Armour and gained publicity in various magazines, including *Parade*, *People*, and *Good Housekeeping*. Furthermore, Abbey was invited to appear on popular TV shows such as *David Letterman* and *Oprah*.

#072 A Chinese man, Jiang Zhongli, has invented a remote kissing device for couples in a long-distance relationship. The device plugs into your phone, and its silicone lips mimic and transfer the movement, pressure, heat, and sound you make to the user's device at the other end of the call. It sells for about $40; some have said it is too realistic and creepy.

#073 You have probably seen the carnival funhouse mirrors that distort different parts of your figure. The mirrors are able to do this because of the way they are curved. There are now mirrors on the market designed to make you look about 10 pounds thinner. The way they work is that they are curved slightly inward as opposed to regular mirrors that are straight up and down.

#074 An invisibility cloak is still the stuff of sci-fi movies, but invisibility shields are currently being made by a UK-based company called Invisibility Shield Co. They make two sizes: a 36" x 24" and a 12" x 8". The larger shield allows the user to blend in with the surroundings and hide in plain sight. They use an optical technology called lenticular lensing which directs light in a way that renders the person behind it appear invisible. You have probably seen this technology used with postcard-size pictures that show a different image depending on the viewer's angle.

More than Trivia *Interesting Stories and Fascinating Facts*

Inventions

#075 Dr. Ali Seifi, a neuroscientist, has invented a straw called the "HiccAway" that he says can eliminate hiccups in 9 out of 10 cases. McDonald's McFlurry straw inspired the HiccAway design, which sells for under $14 on their website.

#076 John Lloyd Wright, though not as famous as his father, Frank, left a lasting legacy by creating Lincoln Logs over 100 years ago. When he was 24 years old, John accompanied his father to Japan to work on the design of Tokyo's Imperial Hotel. Frank needed a structure that could withstand earthquakes, so he developed a system of interlocking timber beams that could sway but not collapse during an earthquake. John was inspired by his father's design and developed the toy cabin construction kit around 1916, naming it after our 16th president. The original Lincoln Log set included instructions on how to build the cabin where Abraham Lincoln grew up.

#077 During the mid to late 1800s, Almon Brown Strowger and his brothers often tried to create a device to do their chores for them. So, later in life, when his business declined, he invented a device to solve his problem. He had a rival in the undertaking business whose wife worked as a telephone operator. He suspected she was diverting calls intended for him to her husband's business. In response, Strowger invented an automatic telephone exchange in 1888 to eliminate the need for manual operators. He received a patent for his invention in 1891 and established the Strowger Automatic Telephone Exchange Company that same year. The company continued to improve its product and obtain new patents. Strowger sold his patents in 1896 for $1,800 (equal to $60,000 today) and his share in the company for $10,000 (equal to $330,000 today). Bell Systems purchased his patents in 1916 for $2.5 million (equal to $63,000,000 today). Afterward, Strowger relocated to St. Petersburg, Florida, where he worked again as an undertaker.

Interesting Stories and Fascinating Facts   **More** than **Trivia**

Inventions

#078 The founder of the chewing gum industry conceived the idea while working for a Mexican leader who chewed a natural gum called chicle. He tried to formulate the gum into rubber for tires, and when that didn't work, he made the chicle into a chewing gum called Chiclets.

#079 Percy Spencer, an employee of Raytheon, accidentally discovered the heating effect of a microwave beam in 1945 when it started to melt a chocolate bar in his pocket while he was working on radar equipment. The first food intentionally cooked in a microwave oven was popcorn; the second was an egg in its shell, which exploded.

#080 *Mugen Puchipuchi* is a bubble wrap keychain toy made by Japanese toy maker Bandai. It mimics the sound that bubble wrap makes when it is popped. It has a double-layer silicone rubber structure that feels like bubble wrap. Incidentally, the original bubble packing material was invented to be a 3-D wallpaper. That didn't work, but it made excellent packing material.

#081 In 1900, a chemist from Switzerland witnessed a wine spill on a restaurant tablecloth, and he decided to create a material that could repel liquid. By 1912, he had succeeded in developing his product and even invented a machine to manufacture it. The chemist named his liquid-proof film cellophane, a combination of cellulose and diaphane. Although cellophane was waterproof, it was not moisture-proof and could not prevent water vapor from passing through. However, a chemist from DuPont was able to create a moisture-proof version of cellophane. Cellophane is used today as the base for self-adhesive tape and packaging for food items, including candy.

Inventions

#082 Though there were over 50 paper clip patents before 1900, the most common paper clip still in use today is the Gem paper clip, which was never patented. Besides holding papers together, paper clips can be used as a lock-picking device in the right hands. National Paper Clip Day is May 29.

#083 Josephine Cochrane received a patent in 1886 for her invention of a dishwasher. Her design was the first to use water pressure to clean the dishes instead of scrubbers. The first dishwashers, priced at $75 to $100, were too expensive for the average household. She was inducted into the National Inventors Hall of Fame in 2006 for her invention.

#084 Austrian-born American film actress Hedy Lamarr was also an inventor. Being self-taught with no formal training, she developed a radio guidance system, along with composer George Antheil, to prevent a torpedo's radio guidance system from being tracked or jammed. They received a patent for their work in 1942, and the U.S. Navy adopted the technology in the 1960s. Today's Bluetooth and GPS technology use some of the same principles of their work, and they were inducted into the National Inventors Hall of Fame in 2014.

#085 Scotsman Alexander Graham Bell is known best for his invention of the landline telephone, but he also had other interests and inventions. He felt his most outstanding achievement was the invention of a wireless phone called the photophone, which transmitted the human voice on a beam of light. When he died in 1922 at his estate in Nova Scotia, Canada, his wife asked guests to celebrate his life and not to wear black to his funeral. When his funeral concluded, all phones in North America were silent for one minute in his honor.

Interesting Stories and Fascinating Facts   **More** than **Trivia**

Inventions

#086   The jar opener is a type of "Gilhoolie" invented in 1952 by Dr. C.W. Fuller, a retired dentist. Fuller held more than a dozen patents related to dentistry and golf. The Gilhoolie patent was his only patent for a kitchen device.

#087   In 1968, a 3M scientist tried to develop a super-strong adhesive but accidentally created a reusable, pressure-sensitive adhesive. Six years later, a colleague had the idea of using the adhesive on paper as a bookmark, and the Post-it Note was born. The yellow color of the original sticky notes was chosen by accident, as the lab where they were developed only had yellow scrap paper to use.

#088   Henry C. Gibson, a farmer and fence company manager from Dardanelle, Arkansas, was granted patent #574,534 in 1897 for his box-style turkey call. This straightforward invention remains widely used by the 2 million turkey hunters who annually seek America's greatest game bird. Turkey calls are used by hunters to lure in these birds, and there are many types of turkey calls to choose from, including those made from turkey wing bones, which were used by Native Americans.

#089   Claude Adkins Hatcher, a prosperous pharmacist from Georgia, made a career change in 1901 when he began working with his father in the wholesale grocery industry. At the time, Coca-Cola was in high demand, and the Hatcher Grocery Company was selling a lot of it. However, a disagreement over wholesale prices led Hatcher to discontinue selling Coca-Cola and create his own soft drink. In 1905, he introduced his first beverage, Royal Crown Ginger Ale. Soon after, he developed Chero-Cola, which was renamed Royal Crown Cola and eventually shortened to RC Cola.

More than Trivia   *Interesting Stories and Fascinating Facts*

Inventions

#090   Colin Pullinger & Sons patented the Perpetual Mouse Trap in 1861. There is a model of it on display at the Museum of English Rural Life (MERL) in Berkshire, UK. In 2016 while on display, the 150-year-old mouse trap caught a mouse without any bait. The museum was not immediately sure what to do with the dead mouse. They considered having it taxidermied and displayed along with the mouse trap.

#091   Prolific inventor Granville Woods received more than 50 patents during his lifetime and was known as "Black Edison." He had to leave school at age 10 to help support his family, and he learned the trades of machinist and blacksmith. Most of Woods' inventions were for trains and streetcars, but he also had other inventions. He invented an egg incubator and received patents for telegraph, telephone, and phonograph improvements. As a successful inventor, other inventors sometimes tried to claim ownership of his patents. He once successfully defended his patent rights against a claim by Thomas Edison. Edison subsequently offered Woods a job, which he declined.

#092   During the late 1800s, a chemist named Robert Augustus Chesebrough visited an oil field in Titusville, Pennsylvania, to witness the newly discovered petroleum. While there, he noticed a by-product of petroleum known as rod wax or petroleum jelly, which workers would remove from the pumping equipment. Despite being considered a nuisance, it was helpful in treating cuts and burns, as it helped alleviate pain and speed up the healing process. Chesebrough patented the process of creating petroleum jelly in 1872, dubbing it Vaseline. He established the Chesebrough Manufacturing Company in 1875, which produced personal-care products. Chesebrough lived to be 96 years old and even claimed to consume a spoonful of Vaseline daily.

Interesting Stories and Fascinating Facts   **More** than **Trivia**

Inventions

#093 In the first century AD, Heron of Alexandria, a Greek mathematician and engineer invented the first vending machine to dispense a set amount of holy water. Apparently, parishioners of the day were drinking too much of the stuff.

#094 Some of the earliest bristle toothbrushes originated in China over 1,100 years ago, made from hog bristles attached to a bamboo or bone handle. This toothbrush spread to Europe, where the Europeans preferred softer bristles made from horsehair.

#095 White-collar workers in Japan often work very long hours, and sleepiness on the job there is a problem, so two Japanese companies have designed a possible solution. They have created a nap box which resembles an aerodynamic water heater that allows you to take power naps during the day. The boxes support the user's heads, knees, and rears so they can nap upright.

#096 There is a remarkable story about an Argentinian engineer named Juan Baigorri Velar, who reportedly invented a rainmaking machine. Although the story is difficult to verify, it is also difficult to dismiss. Velar studied Geophysics at the University of Milan. His device is said to have ended a one-year drought in Santiago, Chile. Additionally, in 1951, his invention produced rain in San Juan, Argentina, where it had not rained for eight years. Velar successfully met a challenge from Alfred G. Galmarini, the director of the national meteorological service, to create rain on a specific date and in a specific area. Unfortunately, little is known about how Velar's device worked, and he declined offers from other countries to purchase it. After Velar passed away in 1972, his rainmaking machine was never found. Interestingly, there was a heavy downpour of rain on the day of his funeral.

More than **Trivia**   *Interesting Stories and Fascinating Facts*

Inventions

#097 The Baby Mop is a onesie for your crawling baby. It is a piece of clothing that has mop-like strands in strategic places on the legs and arms to mop up dirt from your wood or tile floors.

#098 The invention of fortune cookies, as we know them today, is difficult to pin down. Most people nowadays believe they were created by Makoto Hagiwara in 1914 in San Francisco. Hagiwara owned what is now called the Golden Gate Park Japanese Tea Garden, where he served tea and fortune cookies. However, many think fortune cookies were invented by David (Tsung) Jung, who owned the Hong Kong Noodle Company in Los Angeles. He claimed that he stuffed the cookies with Bible scriptures and gave them to unemployed men near his bakery in 1918. In 1983, the debate between the two confectioners came to a head in the Court of Historical Review in San Francisco when their dispute was decided by Judge Daniel M. Hanlon in favor of Hagiwara.

#099 The distinctive copper rivets sewn into denim jeans for the last 150+ years were not invented by Levi Strauss but by one of his customers, Jacob Davis, at his Reno, Nevada, tailor shop. Davis made tents, horse blankets, and wagon covers from cotton duck cloth and denim that he bought from Levi Strauss & Co. in San Francisco. In 1870, a customer asked Davis to make a pair of strong working pants for her husband, and he reinforced the weak points in the seams and pockets with copper rivets. These pants became so popular among railroad workers that he could no longer meet the demand. In 1872, he approached his fabric supplier, Levi Strauss, for financial backing in filing a patent application. The patent was granted in 1873 to Davis and Strauss. In the same year, Davis started sewing a double orange threaded stitched design onto the back pocket of the jeans to distinguish them from his competitors.

Interesting Stories and Fascinating Facts **More than Trivia**

Inventions

#100   George Smith of New Haven, Connecticut, is credited with being the inventor of the modern lollipop. He started making hard candies on a stick in 1908 and trademarked the name lollipop in 1931, after a racehorse named Lolly Pop.

#101   Crapper was a name for a toilet that gained popularity from the work of Thomas Crapper, who popularized flush toilets in 1880s England. He held 9 patents, 3 for toilet-related improvements. There are manhole covers with Crapper's company's name still in Westminster Abbey.

#102   George de Mestral of Switzerland received his first patent at age 12 for a toy airplane. His most well-known patent was for a hook-and-loop fastener, which he named "Velcro." Velcro combines part of the French words *velours* (velvet) and *crochet* (hook). He got the idea after returning from a hunting trip with several burrs stuck to his clothes and his dog's fur. Curious, he examined the burrs under a microscope and eventually figured out how they worked. It took him 10 years to develop a mechanical process that worked, and he received his Swiss patent in 1955.

#103   British doctor and inventor George Merryweather invented a weather-predicting device called the "Tempest Prognosticator" (aka The Leech Barometer). The machine had 12 leeches, each in a pint bottle in a circle around a large bell. When the atmosphere's electromagnetic field changed, the leeches tried to move through a metal tube on top of the bottle they were in, which dislodged a piece of whalebone and caused a small hammer to strike the bell. The more times the leeches rang the bell, the more likely a storm would occur. While interesting, his device never caught on. Perhaps it was too buggy for some.

More than **Trivia**   *Interesting Stories and Fascinating Facts*

Inventions

#104 The French drain, an invention used to divert water, did not originate in France. Instead, it was the invention of Henry Flagg French, an inventor, lawyer, and U.S. assistant secretary of the treasury. He detailed its construction and use in his 1859 book, *Farm Drainage*. He had a son named Daniel Chester French, a sculptor who created the well-known statue of Abraham Lincoln at the Lincoln Memorial.

#105 Otto Frederick Rodwedder, an Iowa native, was a jeweler who owned three jewelry stores in St. Joseph, Missouri. Otto had an idea to create a bread-slicing machine, so in 1916, he sold his jewelry stores to develop his invention. A factory fire destroyed his prototype and blueprints in 1917, but he persevered, finished his machine, and patented it in 1928. He sold his first machine to a friend at the Chillicothe Baking Company in Chillicothe, Missouri. The town of Chillicothe now has an annual Sliced Bread Day, with parades, concerts, and more. Rodwedder's original bread-slicing machine is in the Smithsonian Institution in Washington, DC.

#106 Like many inventions, the snow globe came into being when the inventor tried to invent something else. Austrian Erwin Perzy, who made surgical instruments, was trying to improve the brightness of the light source to use as a surgical lamp. The particles he used in the water-filled flask to reflect light reminded him of snowfall, and he created his first *Schneekugel* (snow globe) in 1900, a model of the basilica of Mariazell in central Austria. Perzy got a patent for his snow globe and started The Original Vienna Snow Globes Company, which continues to this day. The formula for the snow in a Perzy snow globe is a closely guarded trade secret, as its snowfall can last as long as two minutes. The company makes about 200,000 snow globes each year and ships them worldwide.

Interesting Stories and Fascinating Facts   **More** than **Trivia**

Inventions

#107 Eleven-year-old Richie Stachowski invented the Water Talkie, an underwater walkie-talkie, in 1995. He went on to create other pool toys and, in 1999, sold his company to Wild Planet Toys.

#108 The Hoover Company introduced a unique vacuum cleaner in 1954 called the Constellation. The cylinder-type vacuum lacked wheels and floated behind the user on its exhaust. This engineering marvel was discontinued in the mid-1970s but made a resurgence and was sold again from 2006-2009.

#109 In 1916, Sam Born (born in Ukraine as Samuel Bernstein) of California invented the Born Sucker lollipop-making machine, which automatically inserted the stick into the candy. In 1923 he founded the Just Born candy-making company in Brooklyn, New York, that still makes Peeps, Hot Tamales, and Mike and Ike candies.

#110 Frisbee inventor Walter Morrison saw a market for a flying disc after being offered 25 cents for a 5-cent cake pan he tossed around on a California beach in 1937. In 1948 he made plastic discs called the Flyin' Saucer, then later Pluto Platter. He sold the rights to Wham-O in 1957. Wham-O renamed it Frisbee after hearing Yale college students calling them that based on the empty pie tins they were tossing around from the Frisbie Pie Company, which supplied pies to the school with their logo on them. Frisbee's success is attributed to Ed Headrick, Wham-O's general manager, that redesigned the Frisbee and marketed its use as a new sport. When Headrick died and was cremated, his ashes were made into memorial Frisbee discs and given to family and close friends.

More than Trivia   *Interesting Stories and Fascinating Facts*

Inventions

#111 Chapstick was invented in the 1880s. A commercial artist from Virginia designed the logo for it in 1935, which is still used today. He was paid a one-time fee of $15.

#112 The modern-day T-shirt was created by the Cooper Underwear Company in 1904. It was aimed at men with no wives and no sewing skills, and they called it their new bachelor undershirt.

#113 In 1858, Hymen Lipman received the first patent for a pencil with an attached eraser at the end of the pencil. In 1862, Lipman sold his patent to Joseph Reckendorfer for $100,000, who sued pencil manufacturer Faber-Castell for infringement. But in 1875, the United States Supreme Court ruled against Reckendorfer, declaring the patent invalid because his invention was a combination of two already-known things with no new use. Because the patent had been invalidated, anyone that wanted to put an eraser on the end of a pencil could do so. Incidentally, before rubber was discovered to be a good eraser, people used bread crumbs to erase stray pencil marks.

#114 Many people developed innovative food-freezing techniques, but Clarence Birdseye is credited with inventing in 1924 the quick freezing method, which produces the type of frozen foods we know today. The local Inuit people taught him how to ice fish in Canada. He noticed the fish they caught froze almost immediately after being pulled from the water. He discovered that the fish was just as delicious when thawed out months later. From this experience, he theorized that food must be frozen quickly to retain its taste and texture. Birdseye's quick-freezing process ended up creating 168 patents. These patents covered not only the freezing technique but also the packaging, the type of paper used, and related innovations.

Interesting Stories and Fascinating Facts   **More than Trivia**

Inventions

#115 Before the modern nail clipper was invented, people used small knives to trim or pare their nails. Descriptions of nail trimming in literature date back to the 8th century BC.

#116 In the 1920s, the president of B.F. Goodrich requested some slide fasteners for its company galoshes. He coined the term zipper for the boots, not the device that fastened them.

#117 In 1923, Leo Gerstenzang created the first cotton swab called Baby Gays. He later changed the name to Q-Tips Baby Gays, where "Q" stood for quality. He eventually dropped Baby Gays from the name, and the product became Q-Tips.

#118 French hair stylist Alexander Godefroy invented the first hairdryer in 1890. It was a large, seated version that consisted of a bonnet attached to the chimney pipe of a gas stove. Inventor Gabriel Kazanjian patented the first handheld blow dryer in 1911.

#119 Many people and companies contributed to the development of the TV dinner. One of the first variants was in 1945 when they were served on military and civilian airplanes. Frozen dinners grew in popularity, and by 1954, Quaker Foods had sold over 2.5 million frozen dinners. The concept really took hold in 1954 when Swanson's frozen meals appeared. Swanson was a well-known brand that consumers recognized, and they launched a massive advertising campaign for their product. They also coined the phrase, "TV Dinner," which helped transform their frozen meals into a cultural icon.

More than Trivia   *Interesting Stories and Fascinating Facts*

Chapter 3

Human Interest

#120 A six-year-old girl named Madeline has been issued the first-ever preapproved Unicorn license by the Los Angeles County Department of Animal Care and Control. Madeline requested in a letter to the department for official approval to own a unicorn in the county should she ever find one. The department granted the license in December 2022.

#121 Donnie Dunagan served in the Marines from 1952 to 1977, reaching the rank of Major. While in the Marines, he completed three tours in Vietnam and was awarded a Bronze Star and three Purple Hearts. However, he kept a secret while serving – he had been a child actor. He played Peter von Frankenstein in the 1939 Horror movie *Son of Frankenstein* when he was only four. He provided the voice of young Bambi (uncredited) in Walt Disney's 1942 film *Bambi* when he was eight. Before his family moved to Hollywood, they lived in poverty in Memphis. Donnie won a talent contest at 3 1/2, earning him $100 and catching a talent scout's attention. This led to the family's move to Hollywood and Donnie becoming the primary breadwinner, appearing in several films at a young age before joining the Marines.

Human Interest

#122 Olympic discus thrower Piotr Malachowski sold the silver medal he won in 2016 to help raise funds for a 3-year-old boy to pay for surgery to save the child's eyesight.

#123 62-year-old Edwin E. Robinson, from Falmouth, Maine, was struck by lightning on June 1, 1980, restoring his hearing and eyesight. He had been blind and partially deaf since a truck accident in 1971.

#124 On January 8, 2023, which would have been Elvis Presley's 88th birthday, his 1962 Lockheed JetStar plane sold at auction for $234,000. The buyer, James Webb of the YouTube channel "Jimmy's World," plans to convert the aircraft to an RV and tour the country raising money for charities.

#125 On the far side of the moon is a lunar impact crater named "Wan-Hoo," named after a legendary Chinese official named Wan Hu. Because of Chinese advances in fireworks and rockets in the 16th century, Wan Hu built a chair with forty-seven rockets attached to it to launch him into outer space. His plan to become the world's first astronaut fizzled out when there was a huge explosion, and after the smoke cleared, the chair and Wan Hu were gone.

#126 Hody Childress, an elderly farmer of modest means, secretly gave $100 a month for ten years to the local pharmacist to help pay for needed medications for residents in his small town of Geraldine, Alabama. Shortly before he died on January 1, 2023, he knew his time was close, so he told his daughter Tania and asked her to continue his tradition of giving. Tania shared the story of her father's generosity at his funeral, and as the story spread around town, others stepped forward to continue Hody's tradition.

More than Trivia   *Interesting Stories and Fascinating Facts*

Human Interest

#127 The Top Ten most popular last names in the U.S. are 1. Smith 2. Johnson 3. Williams 4. Brown 5. Jones 6. Garcia 7. Miller 8. Davis 9. Rodriguez 10. Martinez.

#128 Merritt Heaton, a farmer from Illinois, was recognized as the oldest active farmer in the state in 1988 at the age of 97. After that, he was invited to appear on *The Tonight Show* with Johnny Carson. He initially declined due to his lack of familiarity with the show and his usual early bedtime. However, he eventually changed his mind and appeared on the show, providing plenty of laughter and entertaining anecdotes from his nearly 100 years of life.

#129 When the National Cathedral in Washington, DC, was renovated in the 1980s, *National Geographic World* magazine sponsored a contest asking young readers to submit designs for new gargoyles. One thousand four hundred entries from kids ages 8 to 13 from 16 countries sent in their ideas. Four of the designs are now carved in stone on the building. The winner was a toothy creature with an umbrella, and the three runner-ups were a raccoon, a pigtailed girl with braces, and Darth Vader.

#130 11-year-old Joe Trofer-Cook of Lincolnshire, UK, does not come from a family of farmers, but that is what he is determined to be. Joe, aka "Farmer Joe," started growing and selling vegetables when he was eight. He used his profits to buy three chickens. He kept saving money and bought four female sheep named Rhubarb, Strawberry, Pumpkin, and Radish, and one male named Basil. He continues to put his profits back into his enterprise. He now rents land locally and owns 37 sheep, 12 chickens, two cows, and a border collie named Spud that he is training to herd his flock. He wakes up at 4 AM to tend his flock and once delivered sheep triplets before going to school.

Interesting Stories and Fascinating Facts   **More** than Trivia

#131 A blood bank company in Stockholm, Sweden, began notifying donors via text message in 2015 when their blood had been used. The company said the updates gave donors a sense that they had made a difference in someone's life.

#132 The wide-scale adoption of duct tape occurred because a mother of two Navy sailors and a factory worker that made ammunition boxes wrote a letter to President Franklin Roosevelt. She was concerned that issues with the wax seal currently used with the boxes would cost soldiers precious time in battle, and she thought that strong waterproof tape would do a better job. A short time later, Johnson & Johnson Company started making Army green tape to seal the ammo boxes. And, of course, our military personnel found many other uses for this new product.

#133 At 34, Robert L. May wrote descriptions about men's clothing as an advertising copywriter for the Montgomery Ward department store in Chicago instead of writing the next great American novel. May was heavily in debt, and his wife was dying of cancer when early in 1939, his boss asked him to write a cheery children's book as a giveaway for their Christmas shoppers. Though May's wife died in late July that year, he finished the book in late August. It was a story about a Christmas reindeer named Rudolph. Montgomery Ward had the softcover "Rudolph the Red-Nosed Reindeer" poem booklet printed, and they distributed 2.4 million copies in the 1939 holiday season. Though Montgomery Ward owned the rights to the story since May wrote it as part of his job, they returned the copyright to him for free. May's brother-in-law, Johnny Marks, wrote the words and music to the song about Rudolph, which Gene Autry recorded. The song became the second-most popular Christmas tune of all time behind "White Christmas."

More than Trivia *Interesting Stories and Fascinating Facts*

Human Interest

#134 In 2016, Grandma Wanda Dench intended to invite her 24-year-old grandson to dinner by text. However, the message was sent to 17-year-old Jamal Hinton instead, as her grandson had a new phone number. They discovered their error, but despite the confusion, Hinton asked if he could still join the dinner, and Dench graciously agreed, stating that feeding everyone is what grandmas do. The two have maintained their friendship and tradition of spending Thanksgiving dinner together each year.

#135 It all started when Boston area antique dealer Scott Wilson found a painting on the curb awaiting the trash truck. He showed it to some friends who suggested he start a collection. The home-based group grew and became so popular that it needed a viewing space. The Museum of Bad Art (MOBA) was born in 1993 with the original treasure he found, *Lucy in the Field with Flowers*, being the signature piece. Other popular pieces besides *Lucy* include *Sunday on the Pot with George* and *Bone-Juggling Dog in Hula Skirt*. Remember that if you visit their website, the art may be offensive to some, like any art.

#136 The 1994 movie, *It Could Happen to You* was inspired by a real-life event from 1984. Robert Cunningham, a 30-year police veteran, was a regular customer at Sal's Pizzeria in Yonkers, New York. His usual waitress was Phyllis Penzo, who had worked there for 24 years. One Friday evening, Cunningham jokingly offered Phyllis a unique tip - they would split the winnings of a lottery ticket where they each picked half the numbers. Phyliss agreed, and they each picked three numbers, and Cunningham went across the street to buy the ticket. The following evening, Cunningham returned to the diner with his wife to tell Phyllis they had won the $6 million lottery. Cunningham and his wife had no regrets about splitting the winnings since Phyllis picked half the numbers.

Interesting Stories and Fascinating Facts **More** than **Trivia**

Human Interest

#137 The Heinz Company plans to gift a new boat to the Dominican-born sailor rescued after surviving 24 days lost at sea with only a bottle of ketchup and a few seasonings to eat. 47-year-old Elvis Francois was repairing his boat in early 2023 when a storm dragged it out to sea, and the Colombian navy later rescued him.

#138 In 1963, Dr. Pepper searched nationwide for a spokesperson to represent their company on various media platforms. They selected Donna Loren, a 16-year-old child performer from Boston, as the Dr. Pepper Girl for five years. Donna's singing voice and energetic personality made her ideal for the role, and she even appeared in four Muscle Beach-themed movies during the 60s. However, her contract with Dr. Pepper restricted her from doing too much in the beach movies because it prohibited her from wearing any outfits that exposed her navel while filming.

#139 John and Elizabeth Reyes inherited a home in Los Angeles in 2022. While renovating the house, they discovered approximately one million copper pennies weighing over 5,500 pounds. While finding cash is usually a good thing, the Reyeses faced a dilemma. Local banks were unwilling to accept that many pennies, and the couple was reluctant to pay the 8% fee charged by coin cashing machines. Though copper has a scrap metal value of approximately $3 per pound, melting coins is illegal. Fortunately, they received several offers for the coins and finalized the sale a few weeks after the story of their find went public. Other people have been lucky in finding valuable coins as well. In 2014, a couple discovered over 1,400 rare, uncirculated gold coins on their rural northern California property worth $10 million. Similarly, a North Yorkshire, UK couple found 264 gold coins from the 1600s and 1700s under their kitchen floor in 2022. They sold the coins at auction for $852,000.

More than Trivia *Interesting Stories and Fascinating Facts*

Human Interest

#140 Ferdinand Cheval (1836-1924), a mail carrier from France, began constructing his Ideal Palace at the age of 43 in southeastern France. He spent 33 years building it, gathering stones for it during his daily mail delivery. Later in life, his exceptional and tireless work on the Palace was recognized by many, including Pablo Picasso. In 1937, Picasso created a *Facteur Cheval* sketchbook with cartoon-style drawings that recounted the story of Cheval and his Palace.

#141 In Queensland, Australia, a mother was planning her daughter's birthday party in 2022. She invited her daughter's friends and ordered several pizzas from their local Domino's Pizza. Sadly, only one person showed up for the party. The heartbroken mom called Domino's to change the large pizza order to only a single pizza. Upon hearing about the little girl's ordeal, Miles, the Domino's shift supervisor, decided to do something special to cheer her up. When the mom arrived to pick up their single pizza, Miles surprised her with a custom-made Chocolate Fudge Brownie and Churro dessert pizza.

#142 If there was ever an inspiring tortoise and hare story, it is the story of 61-year-old sheep farmer Cliff Young that won Australia's 543-mile ultra-marathon race in 1983. Thousands of runners, many under 30, compete in this grueling annual race that can take five days to finish. Missing several teeth and dressed in overalls and work boots, it's safe to say that Cliff stood out from the crowd when he showed up to get his racing number. One reason that Cliff won the race was that he continued running through the night instead of sleeping. Another reason was that his type of running was good for long-distance races. His run was more of a slow shuffle, dubbed the "Young Shuffle," that was later adopted by other runners. Not only did Cliff win the race, but he also beat the race record by 9 hours.

Interesting Stories and Fascinating Facts **More** than Trivia

Human Interest

#143   Jack Reynolds of the UK is the oldest person to ride a zip-line, and he did it on his 106th birthday in 2018.

#144   Mike Ilitch, the founder of Little Caesars Pizza and owner of two professional sports teams, was also a concerned philanthropist. In 1985, he started "Little Caesars Love Kitchen," a traveling restaurant to feed the hungry during natural disasters. After hearing about the 1994 attack on civil rights icon Rosa Parks in her apartment, Ilitch paid her rent for many years so she could live in a safer part of Detroit.

#145   Juliette Lamour, an 18-year-old university student from Ontario, Canada, won $48 million in January 2023 after she bought a lottery ticket for the first time. Her grandfather urged her to buy the ticket after she turned 18, and she had to call her father from the store to know which type of lottery ticket to buy. She plans on fulfilling her dream of becoming a doctor. "Money doesn't define you," Lamour said. "It's the work you do that will define you."

#146   On April 14, 2023, 50-year-old Beatriz Flamini of Spain emerged from a 230-foot deep cave in southern Spain after voluntarily spending 500 days in isolation. The climber and extreme athlete was 48 years old when she entered the darkness and isolation beneath the earth. Her goal was to test her mental fortitude and help researchers understand the effects of extended isolation on the mind and body. She spent her time exercising, drawing, reading, and knitting. She took two cameras down to document her time and experience. In return, her team gave her fresh food, water, and clothing and collected her body waste. She lost track of time after about two months and said the time went by quickly. After leaving the cave, she said she looked forward to her first shower in 500 days and sharing a plate of fried eggs and chips with friends.

More than **Trivia**   *Interesting Stories and Fascinating Facts*

Human Interest

#147 Ann Hodges of Sylacauga, Alabama, is the only person ever hit by a meteorite. It happened in 1954 while she was taking a nap. After the 9-pound meteorite crashed through the roof, it bounced off a radio and hit her on the leg.

#148 74-year-old Geraldine Gimblet of Lakeland, Florida, used part of her life savings to help pay for her daughter's cancer treatment. The day after her daughter's final breast cancer treatment, Geraldine bought a $10 lottery ticket that won her $2 million.

#149 A Bangladesh woman gave birth to a baby boy in February 2019 and then gave birth to twins just 26 days later. This condition, having a double uterus, is called *uterus didelphys* and is not as rare as you think. However, being pregnant in both wombs simultaneously is very rare. Most women that have this condition are not aware they have it.

#150 Roselle, a Labrador Retriever guide dog, was asleep under her owner's desk on the 78th floor of the North Tower when the terrorist attacks on the World Trade Center began in 2001. Roselle guided her owner and 30 others down 1,463 steps through smoke and chaos, and they successfully exited the North Tower after just over an hour. The South Tower collapsed soon after they got out of the building. Roselle then led her owner to a nearby subway station, and the North Tower collapsed a few minutes later. Roselle retired from guiding in 2007 due to medical issues but continued living with her owner until she died in 2011.

Interesting Stories and Fascinating Facts   **More** than **Trivia**

More than Trivia *Interesting Stories and Fascinating Facts*

Chapter 4

Music

#151 Though the Beatles' breakup occurred in 1970, it wasn't legally formalized until 4 years later when John Lennon signed the paperwork terminating their partnership while he was on vacation with his family at Walt Disney World in Florida.

#152 One of Elvis Presley's most noticeable features was his jet-black hair, which was not his natural color. He was born with blonde hair and blue eyes, and even in his early twenties, his hair was sandy blond. However, he chose to dye his hair black because he preferred the appearance.

#153 One of the hottest songs of 1980 was Queen's "Another One Bites the Dust." Ironically, that song, at 110 beats per minute, has been used by CPU instructors to teach their classes the correct speed of chest compressions to use when performing CPR. The American Heart Association recommends 100 – 120 chest compressions per minute. But if you prefer a song with different lyrics, the Bee Gees "Stayin' Alive" has also been used at 103 beats per minute.

Music

#154 The 1966 song, "Eleanor Rigby," is unique in that none of the Beatles play an instrument in the song. Instead, it has a classical string ensemble with four violins, two violas, and two cellos playing a score composed by the Beatles record producer George Martin.

#155 Composer Wolfgang Amadeus Mozart has a round, dark chocolate confection named after him called a *Mozartkugel*. It was initially created in 1890 by Austrian confectioner Paul Furst and was first called the Mozart-Bonbon. The original recipe was a ball of marzipan mixed with pistachio covered in a layer of nougat, then coated in dark chocolate.

#156 Country entertainer Johnny Cash has a new species of tarantula named after him. The *Aphonopelma johnnycashi* was discovered in 2015 near Folsom Prison in California, and the mature male of the species is generally black. As Johnny Cash was called "The Man in Black" and his song "Folsom Prison Blues" brought attention to the prison, it was only fitting that the tarantula was so named.

#157 The 1958 song "The Twist," was written by Hank Ballard and the Midnighters as a "B" side to "Teardrops on Your Letter." Their version hit #28 on *Billboard's* Hot 100 list in 1960. Dick Clark heard about the song and tried to book Ballard on his *American Bandstand* TV show. Ballard was unavailable, so he booked Chubby Checker to perform the song. Checker's cover of the song became a #1 hit in 1960. A new recording of the song 28 years later (1988) by The Fat Boys featuring Chubby Checker was also a hit that reached #2 in the UK and #1 in Germany. In 2014, *Billboard* magazine called it the biggest hit of the 1960s.

More than Trivia *Interesting Stories and Fascinating Facts*

Music

#158 Actor Jackie Chan is also a singer. He has produced over 20 albums, sang over 100 songs in five languages, and received the Best Foreign Singer Award in Japan in 1984.

#159 Country singer/songwriter George Strait is the first artist in the history of *Billboard* magazine to have at least one single record in the top 10 of a *Billboard* chart for 30 consecutive years. Strait has had 61 number-one songs on all country charts and has more number-one hits than any other artist in a single genre.

#160 Saddam Hussein chose Whitney Houston's version of Dolly Parton's song, "I Will Always Love You," to use in his 2002 election campaign. Mayyada Bselees, a Syrian singer, performed the music in Arabic, and it was played from dawn to dusk throughout Iraq until the election was held. Voter turnout was 100%, and he got 100% of the vote (there wasn't anyone else running). Probably a good thing he didn't play the Beatles song, "Revolution."

#161 Though he died in 1959 at 22, Buddy Holly was among the most influential musicians of all time. His music influenced Paul McCartney, John Lennon, Bob Dylan, Mick Jagger, Elton John, Eric Clapton, and many others. Don McLean's 1971 song "American Pie" has a line that refers to Holly's death as "the day the music died." Holly opened for Elvis Presley 3 times in 1955. He wrote and recorded so many songs that his record label released new Buddy Holly music for 10 years after his death. Holly has had many film and musical depictions, including the post-apocalyptic movie, *Six String Samurai* which portrayed him as a guitar-playing samurai traveling to Las Vegas to become the new king of Nevada after the death of Elvis Presley.

Interesting Stories and Fascinating Facts   **More** than **Trivia**

Music

#162 Singer-songwriter Ed Sheeran was accidentally cut on his face in 2016 with a sword by Princess Beatrice, daughter of Prince Andrew, and Sarah, Duchess of York. It happened at a party when their friend, James Blunt, joked that he would like to be knighted. The Princess grabbed a sword to knight Blunt playfully, misjudging the sword's weight and not realizing that Sheeran was standing behind her, and cut Sheeran just below his right eye.

#163 Dale Hawkins, songwriter, music producer, and rockabilly performer who created the hit song "Suzy-Q," received an unexpected offer from Gibson Guitar Company in the early 2000s. They contacted him to express their gratitude for featuring one of their guitars on the cover of one of his earlier albums, which they said helped them sell many guitars. As a gesture of appreciation, they offered to send him any guitar of his choice for free, along with a carrying case. Dale opted for a 6-string acoustic model.

#164 Brian May, lead guitarist of the rock group Queen, has a Ph.D. in astrophysics and, in 2022, was awarded the Stephen Hawking Medal for Science Communication. He is #26 on *Rolling Stone* magazine's list of the "100 Greatest Guitarists of All Time." Though he plays a variety of guitars, much of his guitar work is done on a guitar called the "Red Special" that he and his father built when May was 16, using some household items in its construction. The tremolo arm is made from an old bicycle saddle bag carrier, and the knob at the end is from a knitting needle. The tremolo system springs are valve springs from an old motorbike. The banjolele, a 4-stringed Ukulele-Banjo, is the first instrument he learned to play. He was also trained on classical piano as a child. The songs he wrote for Queen include "We Will Rock You" and "Who Wants to Live Forever."

More than Trivia   *Interesting Stories and Fascinating Facts*

Music

#165 The title of Led Zeppelin's 1971 song "Black Dog" refers to a nameless black Labrador Retriever that wandered around the recording studios while the band was recording their untitled fourth album (*Led Zeppelin IV*).

#166 Dolly Parton has written a song called "My Place in History" and locked it away in a chestnut box called her Dream Box. The box will be opened on January 19, 2046, her 100th birthday. The box is at Dollywood's Dreammore Resort in a glass-enclosed case. The box also contains her book *Dream More* and a piece of wood from her childhood home's front porch.

#167 With only five lines, Japan's national anthem, called "Kimigayo," is the shortest national anthem in the world. The English lyrics are:

May your reign
Continue for a thousand, eight thousand generations,
Until the tiny pebbles
Grow into massive boulders
Lush with moss

#168 The song "Twist and Shout," was initially written by Phil Medley and Bert Berns Russell in 1961. The Top Notes recorded the first version but received little recognition. The Isley Brothers gave the song a new twist, and it was a Top 20 hit in 1962. The Beatles released their version in 1964, which sold over a million copies. It reached number two on the *Billboard* chart during the week of April 4, 1964, when the Beatles held the top 5 spots. Mark Lewisohn, an expert on the Beatles, said it was "arguably the most stunning rock and roll vocal and instrumental performance of all time."

Interesting Stories and Fascinating Facts **More than Trivia**

Music

#169 The song "Yesterday" by the Beatles is one of the most recorded songs in the last 50 years. It was a song that Chuck Berry said he wished he had written. Bob Dylan didn't like the song, but he later recorded his version, accompanied by George Harrison.

#170 The Monkees had four albums in 1967 that spent 29 weeks as the number 1 album on *Billboard's* Number-One Albums list that year. The closest competition was the Beatles, which had only one album, *Sgt. Pepper's Lonely Hearts Club Band* was number 1 for 15 weeks. The other number-one albums that year were one by the Supremes for five weeks, one by Bobbie Gentry for two weeks, and one by Herb Alpert and the Tijuana Brass for one week.

#171 The 1973 song "Smoke on the Water" by Deep Purple tells the true story of their experience in Switzerland, where they went to record in 1971. The night before their recording session, Frank Zappa and the Mothers of Invention were playing at Montreux Casino when someone fired a flare gun at the ceiling, which caused the casino to catch on fire and burn to the ground. The song also has a guitar riff ranked as the #4 "Greatest Guitar Riffs Ever" by *Total Guitar* magazine.

#172 When Dolly Parton's song, "I Will Always Love You," hit #1 on *Billboard's* Hot Country Songs in 1974, Elvis Presley said he wanted to cover the song. Dolly was thrilled until Elvis' manager told her she would have to sign over half of her publishing rights to the song for Elvis to record it. As much as she wanted Elvis to sing her song, she felt she had made the right decision. Dolly turned out to be correct. Whitney Houston's 1992 blockbuster version of the song has sold 20 million copies worldwide and earned Dolly enough royalties to buy Graceland (if it had been for sale).

More than Trivia   *Interesting Stories and Fascinating Facts*

Music

#173 Keyboard player Billy Preston is the only musician to ever receive album credit for playing on a Beatles album. Sometimes known as the "fifth Beatle," he played the organ and electric piano in the 1969 rooftop sessions in the Beatles' final live performance.

#174 John Jacob Miles, born in Kentucky, was a composer and songwriter known as the "Dean of American Balladeers." He influenced artists like Bob Dylan, Joan Baez, and Peter, Paul, and Mary. Some of his better-known songs are "Go 'Way From My Window" and his 1933 Christmas song, "I Wonder as I Wander."

#175 The cymbals that Ringo Starr played with the Beatles on *The Ed Sullivan Show* in 1964 were made by the Zildjian Company. Zildjian was founded in Constantinople in 1623 by Avedis Zildjian, who worked for the court of the Sultan of the Ottoman Empire. In addition to making cymbals for the Ottoman military bands and instruments for churches, they also made finger cymbals for the belly dancers of the Ottoman harem. The company moved from Turkey to the U.S. in 1928 and is today the world's largest cymbal and drumstick maker.

#176 The four members of the band Creedence Clearwater Revival, played together in 1959 as the Blue Velvets. When they signed with Fantasy Records in 1964, the record company's co-owner renamed them the Golliwogs, after a 19th-century children's book rag doll-like character. The band members disliked that name and, in 1967, had the chance to choose their own name. Rejected names included Muddy Rabbit, Gossamer Wump, and Creedence Nuball and the Ruby. This last name was based on band member Tom Fogerty's friend Credence Newball. Eventually, this name led them to choose Creedence Clearwater Revival.

Interesting Stories and Fascinating Facts **More than Trivia**

#177 Before country singer/performer Johnny Cash's music career started, he joined the Air Force in 1950, where he trained as a Morse code operator listening in on Soviet Army transmissions.

#178 Johnny Cash's younger brother Tommy had a 1969 hit "Six White Horses" dedicated to John F. Kennedy, Robert F. Kennedy, and Martin Luther King Jr. and reached #4 on the U.S. Country chart and #1 on the Canadian Country chart. He also had a 1965 single called "I Didn't Walk the Line."

#179 Dexter Holland, lead vocalist, rhythm guitarist, and only remaining original member of the punk rock band the Offspring, received a Ph.D. in molecular biology in 2017. He was valedictorian for his 1984 high school class and a top mathematics student. He said he found math "just as exciting as punk rock."

#180 The world's oldest complete song, including its musical notation, is called the "Epitaph of Seikilos." It was engraved on a tombstone about 2,000 years ago in present-day Aydin, Turkey, near the biblical city Ephesus. The English translation says: : "While you live, shine - have no grief at all - life exists only for a short while - and Time demands his due."

#181 Glen Campbell was a renowned studio musician in Los Angeles before achieving country music stardom. He served as a temporary member of the Beach Boys on their concert tours from December 1964 to April 1965, filling in for Brian Wilson. Bruce Johnston later replaced him as a new member of the Beach Boys. Interestingly, after leaving the Beach Boys in 1972, Johnston sang vocals for several Elton John and Pink Floyd songs.

More than Trivia *Interesting Stories and Fascinating Facts*

Music

#182 Barry Manilow's 1976 number 1 hit song, "I Write the Songs," was not written by Barry Manilow. Bruce Johnston, a former member of the Beach Boys, wrote the song in 1975 after leaving the Beach Boys. Johnston's first appearance on the Beach Boys albums was as a vocalist on their iconic song, "California Girls," in 1965.

#183 The term *Karaoke* is a Japanese compound word that means "empty orchestra." It is composed of the word *kara*, meaning empty, and *oke* (short form of *okesutora*), meaning orchestra. Modern usage refers to singing over pre-recorded music, whereas it originally applied to using any pre-recorded music instead of a real orchestra.

#184 Elvis Presley recorded about 800 songs in his career but didn't write any. However, he did receive co-writing credit for the song "All Shook Up" in one version of the song's origin. Elvis said, "I've never even had an idea for a song. Just once, maybe." He woke up one night after a dream that got him "all shook up." He phoned a friend and told him about it, and by the morning, he had a new song, "All Shook Up."

#185 The Grammy Award recognizes outstanding musical achievement worldwide. Leah Peasall, age 8, was the youngest winner in 2002, who sang with two of her sisters on *O Brother Where Art Thou?*. The oldest winner was 97-year-old Pinetop Perkins in 2011 for the Best Traditional Blues Album *Joined at the Hip*. Group winners and the number of awards include U2 (22), Foo Fighters (15). Further down the list are the Beatles (7) and Simon & Garfunkel (7). The most Grammys won is 31 by Georg Solti, a Hungarian-British conductor. Tied in second place are Quincy Jones and Beyonce, each with 28. Jay-Z and Kanye West each have 24, the most Grammys won by a rapper. Elvis had 3 Grammys.

Interesting Stories and Fascinating Facts **More** than Trivia

Music

#186 A popular rumor started in the late 1960s that Paul McCartney had died in a car accident in 1966 and been replaced by a look alike. So-called clues in Beatles songs and album covers were offered to support this theory. It was suggested that the *Abbey Road* album cover was a funeral procession. Paul was barefooted and out of step because he was dead. Other clues cited were backward messages in some Beatles songs about Paul's death. Analysis of the phenomenon of the "Paul is Dead" rumor continues today.

#187 Singer-songwriter Jake Holmes, a writer of many popular jingles in the 70s and 80s, also wrote songs for Lena Horne and Harry Belafonte. He also co-wrote songs with Bob Gaudio for Frank Sinatra. One of his more famous songs is "Dazed and Confused," which he released in 1967. Jimmy Page adapted and released this song with the Yardbirds and later with Led Zeppelin without giving credit to Holmes. Holmes subsequently filed a copyright infringement suit against Page in 2010, which they settled out of court. Now Led Zeppelin's releases of the song give credit as "Jimmy Page, inspired by Jake Holmes."

#188 Guitar players will sometimes give their favorite guitars a name. Keith Richards has "Micawber," a gift from Eric Clapton. Willie Nelson calls his Martin nylon-string guitar "Trigger," and B.B. King's Gibson electric guitar is named "Lucille." The latter nickname came after King's scary experience in Twist, Arkansas, in 1949. During a show, two men got into a fight over a woman named Lucille, causing a barrel of kerosene to spill and start a fire. Everyone had to evacuate, and King realized he had left his $30 guitar inside. He went back in to retrieve it, and ever since then, he has given all his guitars the name "Lucille" as a reminder to never fight over a woman or run inside a burning building.

More than Trivia   *Interesting Stories and Fascinating Facts*

Music

#189   Emil Richards was an American percussionist who began playing the xylophone at six. He played bongos on the *Mission: Impossible* theme song, finger snaps for *The Addams Family* theme song, and xylophone for *The Simpsons* opening theme song. He also did recordings for Perry Como, Frank Sinatra, Frank Zappa, and Doris Day.

#190   Jake Holmes, aka Jingle Jake, is an American singer-songwriter who wrote several well-known jingles in the 70s and 80s. They include: "I'm a Pepper," for Dr Pepper - "Be all that you can be," for the U.S. Army - "Raise your hand if you're sure," for Sure Deodorant - "Best a man can get," for Gillette - "Come see the softer side of Sears," for Sears.

#191   9-year-old Xabi Glovsky and his dad went to a Bruce Springsteen concert on a school night in 2016. Xabi held up a sign in the audience asking Springsteen to sign a tardy note for him to take to school. Springsteen saw it and asked him and his dad backstage afterward, where he wrote a note for Xabi's teacher asking her to excuse Xabi if he was tardy and why.

#192   Strawberry Field is a Salvation Army-owned property that was a children's home in the Liverpool suburb of Woolton, UK, from 1936 to 2005. It inspired the 1967 Beatles' song "Strawberry Fields Forever" by John Lennon. Strawberry Field was near his home, where he grew up with his Aunt Mimi. John always enjoyed attending the yearly garden party with his Aunt Mimi on the grounds of the children's home, which featured the Salvation Army Band. John would often climb the wall to get onto the grounds at Strawberry Field to play with the children. There were complaints about John doing this, and his Aunt Mimi told him they would hang him if he kept doing that. One of the lyrics in the song says, "nothing to get hung about."

Interesting Stories and Fascinating Facts   **More** than **Trivia**

Music

#193 In 1947, Leo Fender founded the company with his name that made the iconic solid body guitars Fender Telecaster, Fender Stratocaster, and others. Before that, he was an accountant with the California Highway Department. He had been interested in tinkering with electronics from an early age, so when he lost his accounting job, he borrowed $600 and opened a radio repair shop, Fender Radio Service. Though his guitars became some of the most popular in history, Leo Fender never learned to play the instruments he designed.

#194 We have all had an earworm but probably didn't know what to call it. It is also called stuck song syndrome. It's that song lyric you heard somewhere you can not get out of your head. One study says chewing gum helps (not in your ear), but listening to another song is the most common solution. In 1933, E.B. White, author of *Charlotte's Web*, wrote a satirical short story called *The Supremacy of Uruguay*, in which an Uruguayan hotel clerk invents a device that uses an earworm to cause insanity in the masses and allows Uruguay to conquer all the nations of the earth.

#195 In the 1960s and 1970s, a talented and respected group of studio musicians in Los Angeles, known as the Wrecking Crew, played on countless top 40 hits. Despite their contribution, they often went uncredited for their work. The term "Wrecking Crew" was popularized by studio drummer Hal Blaine, but the group was also known as "The Clique" and "The First Call Gang." Several members, including Glen Campbell, Leon Russell, Dr. John (Mac Rebennack), and James Burton (Elvis Presley's guitarist for 8 years), went on to successful solo careers as performers or songwriters. The group was given this name because some older musicians believed that the growing popularity of rock and roll would "wreck" the music industry.

More than Trivia   *Interesting Stories and Fascinating Facts*

Music

#196 There are two explanations for the origin of Neil Diamond's popular 1969 song "Sweet Caroline." The most popular explanation is that it was inspired by John F. Kennedy's daughter, Caroline. Diamond saw a magazine cover of her as a child with her parents, and she was on a horse. A more recent explanation by Diamond said it was about his then-wife Marcia, but he needed a three-syllable name to fit the melody.

#197 "PPAP" (Pen-Pineapple-Apple-Pen) is a 45-second music video by Pikotaro, a fictional singer-songwriter created and portrayed by Japanese comedian Daimaou Kosaka. The official video has over 400 million views, and the single reached #1 on the *Billboard Japan* Hot 100 chart. He later joined Elmo and Cookie Monster on the Japanese edition of *Sesame Street*, singing their version of the song "CBCC" (Cookie-Butter-Choco-Cookie).

#198 Michael Jackson purchased a British broadcasting company, ATV, in 1985 for about $47.5 million. This gave him control over the publishing rights to more than 200 Beatles songs and 40,000 other copyrights. 10 years later, he created a new company by merging his music publishing business with Sony in a deal that earned him a reported $110 million. In 2016, Sony acquired Jackson's share of the company from his estate for $750 million.

#199 When singer/performer Janis Joplin died, she stipulated that $2,500 of her estate be set aside for "a gathering of my friends and acquaintances at a suitable location as a final gesture of appreciation and farewell to such friends and acquaintances." About 200 special guests were invited to participate in this wake at the Lion's Share Club in San Anselmo, California. The invitation said, "Drinks are on Pearl" (Joplin's nickname).

Interesting Stories and Fascinating Facts   **More** than **Trivia**

Music

#200 In 1977, Pink Floyd's album cover prop – a 40-foot-long pig balloon filled with helium – caused chaos at London Heathrow International Airport when it broke loose during the photo shoot for their 10th studio album, *Animals*. The pig had escaped being tied at the nearby Battersea Power Station and drifted over the airport, resulting in the cancellation of numerous flights. Eventually, it landed in a field in Kent, where a farmer discovered it. The farmer was angry because the pig had frightened his cows. Now we know – pigs really can fly.

#201 "In-A-Gadda-Da-Vida" is a 17+ minute song released by the rock group Iron Butterfly in 1968. The album sold over 30 million copies. The song was written one evening by the group's organ player, Doug Ingle. Ingle played the song for Ron Bushy, the drummer, who wrote down the words as Ingle sang. However, Ingle had drank quite a bit of wine by then and slurred his words. The song was supposed to be a love song from Adam to Eve called "In the Garden of Eden." However, because Ingle was slurring his words, Bushy thought Ingle was saying In-A-Gadda-Da-Vida.

#202 The melody for the traditional song, "Happy Birthday to You," comes from an 1893 song called "Good Morning to All." The combination of melody and lyrics in "Happy Birthday to You" first appeared in print in 1912. The Warner/Chappell Music Company claimed to own the copyright for the song after acquiring a company in 1988 that published a piano arrangement of "Good Morning to All." As a result, they began charging and collecting royalties. In 2008, they collected approximately $2 million in royalties. However, in 2015, the copyright was deemed invalid, and in 2016, Warner/Chappell agreed to pay a settlement of $14 million to those who had licensed the song. The song is in the public domain in the U.S.

More than Trivia *Interesting Stories and Fascinating Facts*

Chapter 5

Sports

#203 After MLB (Major League Baseball) had a record number of home runs (6,776) hit in 2019, they instructed Rawlings, who makes the balls, to alter the ball's construction. The change in ball structure reduced the weight by 2.8 grams without changing its size. An independent lab also discovered that the balls hit over 375 feet would fly one to two feet shorter than before. The change worked because 5,940 home runs were hit in 2021 and only 5,215 in 2022.

#204 Rube Waddell (1876-1914) was one of the most dominant pitchers in Major League Baseball and one of the most eccentric players ever. He was fascinated with fire trucks and ran off the field to chase them on multiple occasions. He once left in the middle of a game to go fishing. He disappeared for months during one offseason and was found wrestling alligators in a circus. In 1902 he threw an "immaculate inning," striking out all batters he faced using a minimum of 9 pitches. In 1903 he struck out 302 batters, and in 1904 he had 349 strikeouts. His record of 2 consecutive 300+ strikeout seasons stood for 60 years until Sandy Koufax did it in 1965 and 1966. He was elected to the Baseball Hall of Fame in 1946.

Sports

#205 Kirk Buchner founded the Fictitious Athlete Hall of Fame in 2013. Rocky Balboa of the *Rocky* movie series was the inaugural inductee. Voting in the Fictitious Athlete Hall of Fame is public, and there are three rounds of voting each year.

#206 Golf was banned in 1457 in Scotland because it was thought that young men needed to spend more time training in archery to be ready for a military invasion. The ban was largely ignored, and in 1502, King James IV of Scotland put his royal seal on the game and became the world's first golfing monarch. The game grew in popularity, and today there are over 550 golf courses of different types in Scotland.

#207 55,000 tennis balls are used each year during the two-week-long Wimbledon tennis tournament in the UK. Slazenger makes these tennis balls, and their partnership with Wimbledon dates back to 1902. Often you will see a player serving to ask for 2 or 3 balls, and they examine them and typically throw one back, pocket one, and serve one. They are looking at the fuzziness of the balls as less fuzz means the ball will travel faster when they serve. Each Wimbledon referee has cans of balls under his chair called 3s, 5s, and 7s, depending on how many games they have been used in.

#208 Joel Pritchard, the former Lieutenant Governor of Washington, and two of his friends invented Pickleball in 1965. It is the fastest-growing U.S. sport, with around 5 million players. The play is similar to tennis, though played on a court about one-third the size of a tennis court. A perforated plastic ball is used that is just under 3 inches in diameter and has 26-40 evenly spaced circular holes. Pritchard's wife, Joan, came up with the name because it reminded her of the pickle boat in rowing, where the rowers are chosen from the leftover rowers from the other boats. In the same way, Pickleball uses parts from different racquet/paddle sports.

More than **Trivia** *Interesting Stories and Fascinating Facts*

Sports

#209 The men's marathon race in the 1904 Summer Olympics in St. Louis was one of the most bizarre in history. Fred Lorz was initially declared the winner but was later disqualified. He dropped out of the race after 9 miles, got a 10-mile car ride, and re-entered the race after the car broke down. Thomas Hicks, the eventual winner, wanted to lay down with ten miles left. His trainers prevented him from stopping and, during the last 10 miles, gave him several doses of strychnine (rat poison) mixed with brandy and an egg white. His team carried him over the finish line while he moved his feet like he was still running. Andarin Carvajal, a Cuban postman, entered the race at the last minute after hitch-hiking from New Orleans, where he lost all his money gambling and had to run the race in street clothes. Not eating for 40 hours, he stole 2 peaches from a spectator and ran to an apple orchard to eat apples that turned out to be rotten. He laid down and napped with stomach cramps and, after waking, finished fourth in the race.

#210 16-year-old Betty Robinson Schwartz's talent for running was discovered when a high school coach saw her running to catch a train after school. The coach got her involved in running at school, and in her first official race, a 60-yard dash, she finished second to the U.S. record holder of the 100-meter dash. Her third 100-meter competition was at the 1928 Amsterdam Olympics, where, at 16, she won the gold medal. She was the youngest athlete to win 100-meter Olympic gold. At 19, she was severely injured in a plane crash, and doctors said she would never race again. She did miss the 1932 Olympics and, though unable to bend her knee enough for a regular starting position, was part of the 4 x 100 meters relay at the 1936 Summer Olympics. With Hitler in the stands and the Germans heavily favored, the U.S. team won the race when the Germans dropped the baton giving Robinson her second gold medal. She retired from racing after the Berlin Olympics and worked in a hardware store for many years. She was inducted into the USA National Track and Field Hall of Fame in 1977.

Interesting Stories and Fascinating Facts **More than Trivia**

#211 Usain Bolt, the Jamaican sprinter, winner of eight Olympic gold medals and holder of three world records, has scoliosis. This condition has curved his spine and made his right leg 1/2 inch shorter than his left. Researchers have studied his condition but cannot say whether it has hurt or helped his sprinting career.

#212 British fans set a new record at the 2022 World Cup held in Qatar by not getting arrested. It is the first time there have been zero arrests of UK fans. Some say this is because there was no alcohol available at the stadiums. British officials would not admit that was the only reason but said there might be a connection.

#213 Trent Irwin, a wide receiver for the NFL team Cincinnati Bengals, made commercials when he was young. But when making a Microsoft commercial as a high school freshman caused him to be late for football practice, it had consequences. His coach benched him in the first quarter of their next game, and he told his dad, who also made commercials, that he was done with acting because football was more important.

#214 Glenn Cunningham's legs were severely burned as an 8-year-old boy in a schoolhouse fire in 1917 that killed his brother. Doctors recommended amputating his legs, but his parents decided against it. Against all odds, this determined young boy went on to win a silver medal in the 1936 Olympics in the 1500-meter event. He also set the world record in 1936 for the 800-meter run and a world indoor record for the mile in 1938. While setting all these track records, he also completed his Ph.D. in biology, health, and physical education. He certainly earned his nickname, "The Iron Man of Kansas."

Sports

#215 Rain boots were originally named Wellington boots after the 19th-century Duke of Wellington. There's even a sport named after them called "Welly Wanging" where people compete to throw a Wellington boot as far as possible. The current world record for this sport is around 210 feet.

#216 Most of the Super Bowl rings presented to the winning team have been made by memorabilia company Jostens, possibly the same company that made your high school ring. The NFL pays for 150 rings at up to $7,000 per ring, with the team paying for the rest. It is at the discretion of the winning team how many rings they get and who they give them to. The top rings are "A" level and can cost over $35,000, with some having over 300 diamonds. There are also "B" and "C" level rings of less value to give to practice squad members and whomever the team wants, from the office staff to cheerleaders. Coach Bill Belichick has the most rings with eight, QB Tom Brady has the most as a player with seven, and administrator Neal Dahlen has seven.

#217 James Naismith invented the game of basketball in 1891 while teaching at the Springfield, Massachusetts, YMCA. His boss gave him the task of creating an indoor game to control a rowdy physical education class and help them stay in shape during winter. He also wanted it to be a safer game than other sports. Thinking that placing the goal above the player's head was the solution, he asked a janitor to find him a pair of boxes he could mount. The janitor brought him peach baskets instead, which he used, calling his new game "Basket Ball." The original rules had nine players for each team instead of the five used today. The ball we know today as a basketball had not been invented, so they used a soccer ball. Running with the ball was not allowed, and dribbling was unknown. Passing the ball was the only acceptable way to move it down the court.

Interesting Stories and Fascinating Facts **More** than Trivia

Sports

#218   The Russian shooting team did not compete in the 1908 Summer Olympic Games held in London because they arrived 12 days late. This was because they were still using the Julian calendar. Though Britain had switched to the more up-to-date Gregorian calendar in 1752, Russia didn't make the switch until 1918.

#219   Extreme ironing is a unique activity where individuals take their ironing boards to unconventional places and iron their clothes. This "sport" can occur in various locations, such as mountainsides, in a canoe, while skiing, parachuting, or even underwater. It was invented by Phil Shaw in the UK in 1997 when he came home after work one day and wanted to go rock climbing, except that he had several chores to do, including ironing. So he decided to combine the two activities.

#220   The 1908 song "Take Me Out to the Ball Game," was written by Jack Norworth and Albert Von Tilzer, neither of which had ever attended a ball game. The 1908 version of the song is now in public domain. You may have heard the song's chorus played during the seventh-inning stretch of baseball games, where fans are often encouraged to sing along. Here is the chorus:

Take me out to the ball game,
Take me out with the crowd;
Buy me some peanuts and Cracker Jack,
I don't care if I never get back.
Let me root, root, root for the home team,
If they don't win, it's a shame.
For it's one, two, three strikes, you're out,
At the old ball game.

More than Trivia   *Interesting Stories and Fascinating Facts*

Sports

#221 In 1915, 50-year-old former pro baseball player and manager Wilbert Robinson planned a publicity stunt by catching a baseball dropped from an airplane at 525 feet. But the pilot, Ruth Law, forgot to bring a baseball, so she dropped a grapefruit instead, which made a real mess when it splattered all over Robinson. He started screaming, thinking that he had lost an eye because of the acid from the grapefruit in his eye and the splatter that covered him. But once his teammates started laughing, he realized what had happened. From that time forward, he referred to airplanes as fruit flies.

#222 Ted Williams, one of the greatest hitters in baseball, was also a pilot in World War II. Six years after his discharge, he was called up from a list of inactive reserves to serve on active duty in the Korean War in 1952. He flew 39 combat missions in Korea and often served as John Glenn's (later an astronaut) wingman. Just before he left for Korea, the Boston Red Sox, whom he played baseball for, had a "Ted Williams Day" at Fenway Park. His friends gave him a Cadillac, and the Red Sox gave him a memory book signed by 400,000 fans. At the end of the ceremony, everyone in the park held hands and sang "Auld Lang Syne" to Williams.

#223 One reason the Super Bowl came into being is that the young, upstart American Football League (AFL) gave the long-established National Football League (NFL) some competition by signing some of the top football prospects coming out of college. To resolve the issue, the two leagues agreed to merge after the 1969 season and create a common draft to obtain players. The leagues later became known as the National Football Conference (NFC) and the American Football Conference (AFC). From Super Bowl 1, played in 1967, until Super Bowl 57 in 2023, the NFC has edged out the AFC by 29 to 28 wins. Super Bowl 1 was the only time the game did not sell out, even though the average ticket price in 1967 was $12.

Interesting Stories and Fascinating Facts　　More than Trivia

#224 Fans sometimes hold up a card with the letter "K" after a baseball player strikes out. Englishman Henry Chadwick, the "Father of Baseball," invented this abbreviation. He had already used "S" to indicate a sacrifice at bat, so he used the last letter of "struck" to represent a strikeout. "K" represents a strikeout where the batter swung and missed the third strike, while a backward "K" means the umpire called the third strike without the batter swinging.

#225 Martial arts has a ranking system designated by the student's belt color. There are some color variations, but the rank order, from lowest to highest, in Taekwondo by the American Taekwondo Federation (ATA) is White, Orange, Yellow, Camouflage, Green, Purple, Blue, Brown, Red, and Black. Once the black level is attained, there are 10 levels of the black belt that can be achieved. It takes from 3 to 5 years to earn the first-level black belt. Very few people reach the 10th-level black belt, which takes a minimum of 57 years. There are about 300 Taekwondo Grand Masters (9th-level black belt), most of whom live in Korea.

#226 With a lifetime batting average of .243, Moe Berg was never more than an average baseball player in the 15 seasons he played in the major leagues. But known as "the brainiest guy in baseball," he was one of the more interesting people to ever play the game. He spoke several languages, read 10 newspapers daily, graduated from Princeton University and Columbia Law School, was an avid world traveler that later became a spy for the United States government, and was awarded the Medal of Freedom by President Harry Truman. His baseball card is the only one on display at CIA headquarters. He is the subject of two films: *The Catcher Was a Spy* and *The Spy Behind Home Plate*.

More than Trivia   *Interesting Stories and Fascinating Facts*

Sports

#227 As a boy, Stanley Roger Smith was turned down for a ball boy job at a Davis Cup tennis event because he was thought to be too clumsy. He went on to become the number 1 tennis player in the world. In 1971, he won the U.S. Open, and in 1972 he won the Wimbledon Championship.

#228 At 3 feet 7 inches tall, Eddie Gaedel was the smallest player to appear in a Major League Baseball game. He only went to bat once in 1951, when he was walked on four consecutive balls. As you can imagine, he had a small strike zone to pitch to. His jersey, bearing the uniform number "1/8", is displayed in the St. Louis Cardinals Baseball Hall of Fame and Museum.

#229 53-year-old grandfather Mark Waldron often worked out at the gym before he got the coronavirus and pneumonia in 2020 and almost died. While recuperating, he first began learning about arm wrestling. After his recovery, he started training to be an arm wrestler. In 2023, three years after starting the sport, he represented Great Britain at the European Championships and won the gold medal.

#230 For the first time in 146 years, Wimbledon has changed its women's tennis dress code. Beginning in 2024, ladies can wear dark-colored undershorts. Some players felt that Wimbledon's all-white rule was too strict, and players have pushed the boundaries of the rules over the years. Andre Agassi didn't play at Wimbledon between 1988 and 1990 due to his objection to the dress code. The all-white rule means all-white, not off-white or cream colors. That rule also applies to any clothing item worn – shoes, headbands, wristbands, etc. There is no official dress code for spectators, but some guidelines exist. Prohibited items include dirty sneakers, torn jeans, and shirts with political or offensive statements.

Interesting Stories and Fascinating Facts   **More** than **Trivia**

#231   Here are two of the longest non-scoring plays in NFL history. In 2011, Percy Harvin of the Minnesota Vikings returned a kickoff 104 yards before being tackled at the 3-yard line. In 2018, Marcus Maye of the New York Jets returned an interception for 104 yards before being tackled at the 1-yard line.

Chapter 6

Places

#232 A new neighborhood, Serenity Place, is being built in Henderson, Nevada, with streets named after Pokémon characters. Imagine living on a street with a name like Squirtle Lane, Jigglypuff Place, or Snorlax Lane.

#233 Churchill, Manitoba, Canada (pop. 8700) is the "Polar Bear Capital of the World." The town of Churchill, on the western shore of Hudson Bay, is in the immigration path of the bears. The bears typically leave Hudson Bay in the summer when the ice melts. Just before the Bay begins to freeze again in October or early November, the bears move toward the coast, waiting for the Bay to freeze so they can hunt for food, primarily ringed seals. The best way to view the bears around Churchill is with a Polar Bear tour operator and their specialty Tundra-equipped vehicles. Residents can call a Polar Bear Alert Program hotline if an errant polar bear wanders into town. A staff member will try to scare the bear away, and if that doesn't work, they will tranquilize it and take it to the Polar Bear Jail. This jail is a former military aircraft hangar with several 12-foot x 16-foot cells. About 50 bears are put in jail per year and kept there for up to 30 days before returning to the wild.

Places

#234 The post office in Romance, Arkansas (pop. 1,772) sends out over 10,000 cards each Valentine's Day that people from all over the world have sent to them to mail out with the unique Romance postal cancellation stamp on the envelope.

#235 The Singing Drain Pipes in Dresden, Germany, becomes a musical instrument when the rain begins to fall. The system of gutters and drains is an artistic experiment located on the side of a building in a courtyard of the student district. It is part of a complex of five courtyards called the *Neustadt Kunsthopassage* (Art of Courtyards).

#236 The Dog Bark Park Inn, known by local residents as "Sweet Willy," is a two-bedroom bed and breakfast in Cottonwood, Idaho, shaped like "The World's Biggest Beagle." You will also find a Chainsaw Folk Art / Gift Shop at the Dog Bark Park featuring over 60 breeds of carved wooden dogs. They have been featured on *The Ellen Show* and *The Today Show* and were named one of the "Top 20 Most Fun & Exciting Places to Stay" by *The London Times*.

#237 Tsovkra-1 (there is another Tsovkra nearby) is a small village located on Russia's western side of the Caspian Sea. The village is unique because most residents can walk a tightrope; it has been a tradition there for over a century. Despite the population dwindling from 3,000 in the 1980s to less than 400 today, school children still study tightrope walking. According to a legend, young men from the village strung a rope from Tsovkra-1 to another village in the valley to save time by tightrope walking across to meet and court women. Although the true origin of this custom remains a mystery, some villagers went on to perform in Soviet circus shows during the latter half of the 20th century.

More than Trivia *Interesting Stories and Fascinating Facts*

Places 73

#238 One of the most unusual jobs in the world falls to four women who run the post office and gift shop in Antarctica. Other tasks at the "Penguin Post Office" is counting the penguin population and mailing out about 80,000 postcards each year to people from all over the world that want their postcards postmarked from Antarctica.

#239 Mill Ends Park in Portland, Oregon, is currently the world's smallest park. It's only 2 feet across and has just one tree. The park's location was supposed to be a site for a light pole, but the pole never showed up. Instead, a newspaper columnist named Dick Fagan planted flowers there and called it "Mill Ends" after his column. Legend has it that Fagan once saw a leprechaun digging in the park's location and was granted a wish by the creature. He wished for his own park but didn't specify the size, so he ended up with the tiny Mill Ends Park. Some say that leprechauns play in the park at night and can only be seen by humans on St. Patrick's Day during a full moon, but only by children carrying four-leaf clovers as gifts. The next full moon on St. Patrick's Day will be March 17, 2041.

#240 The town of Rjukan, Norway, is located in a deep valley surrounded by steep mountains. It has about 3,400 people, but what it doesn't have, from September to March, is sunshine. So, in 1928, the town built a gondola to transport the townspeople to the mountains so they could enjoy the sunshine. An earlier idea from 1913 to supply sunshine to the town was to place mirrors at the top of the mountains to reflect the sun. Unfortunately, the technology wasn't available at the time to do that. But that idea came up again in 2005, and in 2013, 100 years after the original idea, the sun mirrors became a reality. There are 3 computer-driven mirrors on a mountain about 1,500 feet above the town. The mirrors reflect enough of the sun to give a little more than 1/6 of an acre of light to the town square.

Interesting Stories and Fascinating Facts　　**More than Trivia**

Places

#241 Pig Beach, home of the swimming pigs, is a small island in the Bahamas, and its only inhabitants are about 20 feral pigs. No one knows how the pigs got there, but the swimming pigs are a popular tourist attraction.

#242 Hay-on-Wye in Wales has been called the "town of books" or the "used book capital of the world." With a population of about 1,600, it is a destination for book lovers in the United Kingdom and contains over 20 bookshops.

#243 Poland has a grove of 400 oddly-shaped pine trees called "The Crooked Forest." There is no verifiable reason why they have grown this way. Just above ground level, each tree bends sharply to the north for about 3 to 6 feet, then curves back upright. The curved pine trees are surrounded by a forest of straight pine trees. The forest is understandably a popular tourist attraction.

#244 Talkeetna, Alaska, (pop. 1,055), differs from your average Alaskan town. They had an honorary mayor for 20 years named Stubbs, who was a cat. They used to have an annual Moose Dropping Festival celebration until it was canceled in 2009. At some point, PETA got wind of the festival, thinking they were dropping moose out of helicopters. The town finally made PETA understand that moose droppings (dung) were dropped out of a helicopter, not the actual moose. Then there is the annual Wilderness Woman Contest held each December and organized by the Talkeetna Bachelor Society. The contest includes at least three timed events highlighting the skills that a Talkeetna bachelor would find most desirable in a woman, such as hauling firewood, driving a snow machine, climbing a tree, or fetching water. But if you prefer normal outdoor activities such as rafting, hiking, camping, hunting, or fishing, you can do that too.

More than Trivia   *Interesting Stories and Fascinating Facts*

Places

#245 Supai, Arizona, is the most remote community in the contiguous U.S. Its only access is by mule, helicopter, or on foot, and mail is carried in and out by mule. Supai is within the Grand Canyon, has a population of about 200, and there are no automobiles in the community. It is the capital of the Havasupai Indian Reservation.

#246 Chicago has long been known as the Windy City but not for the reason that you think. Another popular theory for the nickname's origin dates back to 1890 when Chicago competed with New York for hosting the 1893 Worlds Fair. Some felt that the residents and politicians of Chicago were "full of hot air" due to their boasting and bloviating about their city.

#247 There are two U.S. cities that claim to be the "Granite Capital of the World" - Elberton, Georgia and Barre, Vermont. Geologists say that Elberton's granite deposit is 35 miles long, 6 miles wide, and 2-3 miles deep (525 cubic miles). Barre's granite deposit is said to be 4 miles long, 2 miles wide, and 10 miles deep (80 cubic miles). Elberton's granite is called blue granite and Barre's granite is called Barre Gray.

#248 The Poison Garden is part of the 12 acres of gardens at the Alnwick Garden in Alnwick, Northumberland, England. All of the gardens, including the Poison Garden, were the brainchild of Jane Percy, the Duchess of Northumberland, who wanted something different from other gardens. The Poison Garden features about 100 toxic, intoxicating, and narcotic plants, including those that produce strychnine, ricin, hemlock, Deadly Nightshade, and others. The boundaries of the Poison Garden are kept behind iron gates, and the most dangerous plants are kept within giant cages. Though visitors are prohibited from smelling, touching, or tasting any plants, some have fainted from inhaling toxic fumes while walking in the garden.

Interesting Stories and Fascinating Facts **More than Trivia**

Places

#249 In London, the local taxis are called "hackney" or "hackney carriage." To become a licensed driver of these taxis, one must pass a challenging test known as "The Knowledge." This test covers 25,000 streets, 320 standard routes, and various points of interest. On average, it takes about 34 months to pass this test, which has remained essentially unchanged since its inception in 1865.

#250 The Roman Colosseum, constructed in 80 AD, is the world's biggest amphitheater, with a seating capacity of up to 80,000 individuals. The arena measures 272 feet by 157 feet and features a wooden floor covered in sand. An underground structure exists beneath it, comprising tunnels, cages, and lifts to facilitate the movement of people, animals, and props to and from the arena and the Colosseum.

#251 The Gate Tower Building in Osaka, Japan, is a 16-floor office building notable for a highway offramp that passes through the building's fifth, sixth, and seventh floors. The highway passes through the building as a bridge and does not contact the building. It is held up by supports next to the building and surrounded by a structure to protect the building from noise and vibration. It was completed in 1992.

#252 Rednaxela Terrace is a pedestrian-only street in Hong Kong whose name is a reversed spelling of Alexander. There is no official reason for this transposition. Still, it is believed that the road was part of the property owned by a Mr. Alexander. Rednaxela is an understandable transposition of the English name Alexander since the Chinese language was typically written right to left at the time. Another explanation is that the name is linked to abolitionist Robert Alexander Young, who was known to have used the name Rednaxela in his 1829 work *Ethiopian Manifesto*.

More than Trivia   *Interesting Stories and Fascinating Facts*

Places

#253 Beneath the streets of Cincinnati, Ohio, lies an abandoned subway system that spans over 2 miles. Back in the early 1900s, the city had ambitious plans to create a 16-mile loop, but due to various issues, the project was never completed. Despite efforts to bring the project back to life, the only visitors to the subway system today are the homeless and a handful of urban explorers.

#254 A massive clock in front of the Nittele Tower in Tokyo, Japan, entertains visitors 4 or 5 times a day with its cuckoo-clock-type array of cannons, blacksmiths, boiling teapot, and more. The clock is three stories tall, 60 feet wide, and weighs over 20 tons. It springs into action every day at noon, 3 PM, 6 PM, and 8 PM and on the weekends at 10 AM Saturday and Sunday. It also keeps time.

#255 Japan's Nishiyama Onsen Keiunkan Hotel is the oldest hotel in the world. It was founded in 705 AD by Fujiwara Mahito, son of an aide to Japanese Emperor Tenji, the 38th Emperor of Japan. The hotel has been owned and operated by 52 generations of the same family. The hotel is at the base of the Akaishi Mountains, where the hotel's natural hot water flows directly from the local Hakuho Springs. Each of the 37 rooms had private hot spring baths added in 2005.

#256 The International Spy Museum, located in Washington, DC, provides a detailed account of the history of espionage. It boasts the world's most extensive collection of international espionage artifacts exhibited to the public. Unique items on display include a printing plate utilized by the Nazis during World War II to forge British currency and a Lipstick Pistol used by KGB operatives during the Cold War. Additionally, the museum features the Aston Martin DB5 car used in the James Bond movie *Goldfinger*.

Interesting Stories and Fascinating Facts   **More than Trivia**

Places

#257 Just Room Enough Island, aka Hub Island, is in the Thousand Islands chain in north central New York. It is only about one-thirteenth acre but has a house, a tree, bushes, and a small beach. The Sizeland family bought it in the 1950s because they wanted a holiday getaway.

#258 One of the best views in Tokyo, Japan, is from the 40-foot-high replica of New York's Statue of Liberty in the Odaiba area of Tokyo. This Odaiba Statue of Liberty has a striking view of Tokyo Bay and the Rainbow Bridge in the background. In addition to this one in Odaiba, other Statue of Liberty replicas are scattered throughout Japan.

#259 A popular tourist destination in the Netherlands has no roads or cars - only walking paths and canals that you travel by boat. The town of Giethoorn (pop. 2,805) is known as the Venice of the Netherlands. In 2015, Giethoorn was chosen from 182 contenders to be a property on the Monopoly Here & Now: World Edition board. Almost 4 million people worldwide cast votes for their favorites to be one of the new property spaces, and Giethoorn was one of the cities chosen.

#260 SubTropolis is a 1,100-acre industrial park inside the former Bethany Falls limestone mine in Kansas City, Missouri. It is built into the bluffs above the Missouri River and is accessible by roads and railroad tracks. The facility's massive grid of large tunnels maintains a constant 68 degrees of temperature. Over 50 tenants utilize the space, including the U.S. Postal Service, which stores hundreds of millions of stamps there. Thousands of reels of movie films such as *The Wizard of Oz* and *Gone With the Wind* are stored there to prevent degrading. In the early '70s, Ford Motor leased 25 acres to store the surplus Ford Maverick cars they had. It also contains a certified 5K, and 10K course used each winter for the Groundhog Run.

More than Trivia   *Interesting Stories and Fascinating Facts*

Places

#261 There is a reason why the World War II cargo ship, the SS *Richard Montgomery*, remains sunken in the waters of the Thames River, where it empties into the North Sea, about 50 miles east of London. In August 1944, the ship went down with 1,500 tons of explosives on board, which remain unexploded. There are concerns that if the explosives detonate, it could cause significant damage both upriver and in the nearby town of Sheerness, Kent.

#262 Many towns take pride in the famous people born there – in the past. Riverside, Iowa, takes a different approach because of one famous person to be born there in the future – James T. Kirk. According to the canon of *Star Trek* material, the famous captain of the Starship *Enterprise* will be born in Riverside, Iowa, on March 22, 2228. Riverside has a Star Trek Museum officially named "The Voyage Home Riverside History Center." Walter Koenig, who played Commander Chekov in the *Star Trek* series, was part of the ribbon-cutting ceremony for the museum when it opened in 2008.

#263 The Eiffel Tower (The Iron Lady) was constructed for the 1889 World's Fair in Paris. Its name derives from Gustave Eiffel, whose company designed and built the tower. The tower undergoes painting every seven years with 60 tons of paint to prevent rusting. The tower has three shades of paint, with the lighter shade at the top and the darker at the bottom. The color changed from its original reddish-brown to bronze in 1968 and will be painted gold for the 2024 Summer Olympics in Paris. Since its inception, over 300 million people have visited the tower. The Eiffel Tower has inspired similar towers in various parts of the world, including the Tokyo Tower in Japan, several scale models in the U.S., two in China, and one in Mexico. Although the tower's height has changed over the years due to an antenna change, it currently stands at 1,083 feet tall and was the world's tallest structure when built in 1889.

Interesting Stories and Fascinating Facts **More than Trivia**

Places

#264 Nagoro Doll Village is a small town in southern Japan with less than 30 residents, but it has over 400 scarecrow-type dolls. Some dolls resemble current or former residents, and others are various characters scattered around. This practice started in the early 2000s when the family of Tsukimi Ayano moved back to the village she left as a child. Tsukimi has made about 400 dolls herself, but others have also started making dolls. Some dolls include a man fishing in a river, children in a classroom, a group at a bus station, and others. It is now a tourist attraction.

#265 Though they both have around 1.4 billion people, India is estimated to surpass China in 2023 as the most populous country in the world. India's population growth rate is almost three times higher than China's, with an annual increase of 1% compared to China's 0.357%. In terms of population density, India has 1,200 people per square mile, while China has 400. India's life expectancy in 2019 was 69.1 years, compared to China's 75.8 years. India has a younger population, with a median age of 26.7 years in 2019, compared to China's median age of 37 years.

#266 In 1973, two writers from *The Des Moines Register* decided to cycle across Iowa and write articles about their six-day trip along the way. It was a popular event; others wanted to share the experience that didn't get to the first time. It is now an eight-day event with seven days of riding, starting at the Missouri River on Iowa's western border and ending at the Mississippi River on Iowa's eastern edge. The route averages 468 miles and changes yearly, as do the eight towns that host overnight lodging. This is a ride and not a race. Though thousands participate annually, space is limited, and you must register beforehand. Check their website for complete details. (*www.ragbrai.com*)

More **than** Trivia   *Interesting Stories and Fascinating Facts*

Places

#267 Post Office Bay is a small outdoor area on Floreana Island in the Galápagos Islands, about 800 miles west of Ecuador. People leave unstamped mail to be delivered by whoever is going in that direction. With its fresh water supply, Floreana Island has been a favorite stopping-off place since the 19th century for whaling ships. Visitors still place cards and letters in the barrel without any postage. Visitors sift through the letters and cards to deliver them by hand, or in some situations, someone places a stamp on it and drops it in the next standard mailbox they come across.

#268 The longest hiking trail in the U.S. goes coast to coast and is called the American Discovery Trail. It splits into a northern (4,834 miles) and southern (5,057 miles) route in southeast Indiana and connects back up in Colorado. It runs from Delaware to California, and horses can be ridden on most of the trail. It passes through 14 national parks and 16 national forests and connects with 34 national recreational trails. Husband and wife team Ken and Marcia Powers were the first to complete the trail in one continuous walk. In 2005, they completed the southern route in about 7 1/2 months averaging 22 miles a day.

#269 The Hang Son Doong Cave in Vietnam is a natural wonder that ranks among the largest caves in the world. Its central passage extends over 3 miles, is 600 feet tall, and 500 feet wide. With stalagmites towering over 200 feet, it could house multiple forty-story skyscrapers. The cave includes jungle areas with trees reaching up to 150 feet in height. Tours are limited to 10 people for safety, and only 1,000 visitors are permitted annually. Each tour requires more than 25 guides, porters, and safety advisors, and the cost per person is $3,000. The "cave of the mountain river" tour is not for the faint of heart. It lasts four days and three nights and is considered one of the world's top adventure experiences.

Interesting Stories and Fascinating Facts   **More** than **Trivia**

Places

#270 In Wuppertal, Germany, a pedestrian/bicycle bridge was painted in 2011 to look like it was made of colorful Lego blocks. The painting took 13 days and was done by graffiti and street artist Martin Heuwold.

#271 The Leaning Tower of Pisa in Italy is 185 feet tall on the high side and leans almost 4 degrees. The building leans because it was built on soft soil. However, that same soft soil has helped the building survive four strong earthquakes since 1280 because the soft soil does not transfer the intensity of the earthquake ground motion to the building.

#272 The towns of Boring, Oregon, and Dull, Scotland, established a Sister Cities partnership in 2012, despite their small populations of 8,000 and 84 respectively. Bland, New South Wales, Australia (pop. 6,000) joined the coalition in 2014 to form "The League of Extraordinary Communities." *The Scotsman* newspaper calls this union the "Trinity of Tedium."

#273 Monaco, or the Principality of Monaco, has less than 1 square mile of land that houses about 38,000 residents making it the most densely populated country in the world. It is also one of the most expensive and wealthiest places in the world. It is located on the French Riviera in Western Europe bordered by France's Alpes-Maritimes on three sides, with one side bordering the Mediterranean Sea. It is a popular tourist destination due to its mild climate, beautiful scenery, and the Monte Carlo Casino. It has recently become a major banking center and is famous as a tax haven. Over 30% of the residents are millionaires. It also hosts the annual street circuit motor race, the Monaco Grand Prix. Its population density is 48,466 people per square mile, vastly greater than the roughly 6 people per square mile that the U.S. state of Wyoming enjoys.

More than Trivia   *Interesting Stories and Fascinating Facts*

Places

#274 Liechtenstein, one of the smallest countries in the world with 38,000 people, produces 20% of all false teeth sold worldwide. Ivoclar Vivadent is a company with 3,500 employees worldwide that ships dental products from Liechtenstein to 130 countries, including 60 million sets of false teeth annually.

#275 Finland is a great place to view the Northern Lights 200 nights out of the year. There are several locations to stay and view the lights, but one of the more interesting ones is the Kakslauttanen Arctic Resort. There are several 2-person glass igloos where you can enjoy the Northern Lights while lying in bed. The 2-person igloos have a toilet, and there are 4-person igloos with their own shower. There are also cabins available with great views of the lights.

#276 In the 1600s, missionary Andres Lopez notified the Pope of a city in the Peruvian Amazon called Paititi that contained vast treasures of gold, silver, and jewels. Though the Vatican kept Paititi's location a secret, over 15 expeditions in the past 100 years have tried to find the "Lost City of Gold." The first such expedition in 1925 was British explorer Percy Harrison Fawcett who is said to have inspired the character Indiana Jones, and the idea for the movie *The Lost City of Z*.

#277 Some of the more unique town names in the U.S. include Nothing, Arizona - Nowhere, Colorado - Greasy Corner, Arkansas - Fluffy Landing, Florida - Santa Claus, Indiana - Embarrass, Minnesota - Money, Mississippi - Licking, Missouri (not to be confused with French Lick, Indiana where NBA legend Larry Bird went to high school) - Funk, Nebraska - Buttzville, New Jersey - Truth or Consequences, New Mexico - Boogertown, North Carolina - Zigzag, Oregon - Difficult, Tennessee - Jot Em Down, Texas - Bread Loaf, Vermont - and Disco, Wisconsin.

Interesting Stories and Fascinating Facts **More** than **Trivia**

Places

#278 The Canary Islands are not named after those cute little yellow birds but after dogs. The Latin name for the islands, *Canariae Insulae*, means "islands of the dogs" because one of the larger islands has many large dogs. This is also depicted in their coat of arms which has two dogs.

#279 Colma, California, is known as "The City of Souls." The number of dead there outnumbers the living by 1,000 to 1. Colma is 11 miles southwest of San Francisco, with a 2020 population (above ground) of 1,507. In 1900, San Francisco ceased allowing burials in the city and county, and in 1914, sent eviction notices to all cemeteries to remove all bodies and monuments. The cemeteries relocated to nearby Colma, which today has about 1.5 million people buried across fifteen cemeteries. Some notable people buried in Colma include William Randolph Hearst, Willie McCovey, Wyatt Earp, Levi Strauss, and Joe DiMaggio.

#280 Most of Whittier, Alaska's 272 residents, live in Begich Towers, a 14-story building built in 1957 as military barracks. It now is a town under one roof with condos, a post office, a grocery store, a police station, a medical clinic, a laundromat, a church, city offices, and more. In 1964 it survived the most powerful earthquake ever recorded in North America. Before 2000, the only way to get to Whittier was by boat or rail. The 2.5-mile railroad tunnel under Maynard Mountain was redesigned in 2000 as a single-lane highway and railway. The tunnel allows one-way traffic and reverses the direction of the allowed traffic flow every 30 minutes until it closes each night at 10:30 PM. The 50 or so kids attending Whittier School have a tunnel connecting them to the Begich Towers. There's little for social life here, but if you like the outdoors, there's plenty to see. Outsiders sometimes call the Whittier lifestyle weird, but some residents consider their town magical.

More than **Trivia** *Interesting Stories and Fascinating Facts*

Places

#281 Monowi is an incorporated .21 square mile town in northern Nebraska with a population of one, Elsie Eiler. The town has a bar, a library, and four street lights.

#282 The small town of Nazaré, Portugal, is a popular surfing destination and home to several world surfing records. Due to the 16,000 feet deep underwater Nazaré Canyon just off the coast, 100-foot high waves are not uncommon. In 2020, Sebastian Steudtner, a German surfer, rode a massive 86-foot wave in Nazaré.

#283 Calico Rock, Arkansas, is unique as it has an authentic ghost town within its city limits. Gunfights were once common over a hundred years ago, like many frontier towns in America. However, today most structures, such as the former jail, barbershop, grist mill, tavern, hardware store, blacksmith shop, and feed store, are boarded up and overgrown, and the land is privately owned. Visitors can take walking tours and go inside the former jail.

#284 Since the 1940s, Gibsonton (Gibtown), Florida, has been home to off-season circus performers. The Monkey Girl, The Lobster Boy, The Half Woman, The Rubber-Faced Man, and others lived in Gibtown without being stared at or ridiculed. Local laws and customs were adapted for the unique residents. The local post office had a low counter for the little people living there, and there were special zoning laws to allow some residents to keep elephants, tigers, or monkeys in their yards. Times have changed, and interest in sideshow acts has dwindled, but circus performers still live there and their descendants. Gibsonton is home to the largest showmen's association in the U.S. The dues from the 4,500 members help to pay for a local circus museum and housing costs at a local retirement village for aging and retired circus performers.

Interesting Stories and Fascinating Facts   **More than Trivia**

Places

#285 The city of Afton in western Wyoming (pop. 2,172) boasts the world's largest arch made of elk antlers. This impressive structure stretches 75 feet across the four lanes of U.S. Highway 89, comprises 3,011 elk antlers, and weighs 15 tons.

#286 Between 1887 and 1930, the Midwest had 34 "Corn Palaces" to advertise its region and products. The last remaining Corn Palace in Mitchell, South Dakota, is a popular tourist attraction drawing 500,000 visitors annually. This multi-purpose facility can accommodate 3,200 people and hosts numerous events like the annual Corn Palace Festival, Corn Palace Stampede Rodeo, and Corn Palace Polka Festival. Additionally, the Dakota Wesleyan University basketball team plays in the Corn Palace. Local farmers grow twelve shades of corn to create the corn murals on the building's exterior.

#287 The Greenbrier Resort in White Sulphur Springs, West Virginia, is one of the country's most exclusive and luxurious resorts. However, it kept a secret for over thirty years. The U.S. government constructed a secret bunker beneath the resort during the time leading up to the Cuban Missile Crisis between 1959 and 1962. The bunker served as an emergency relocation center for the U.S. Congress. This initiative was called Project Greek Island and codenamed "Casper." The bunker featured a dormitory, hospital, kitchen, and broadcast center. The resort's renovation work was used as a cover-up to conceal the bunker's construction, which blended in with the resort's above-ground facade, including four blast doors, one weighing 25 tons. Government employees, disguised as hotel staff, were responsible for maintaining the bunker's facilities. *The Washington Post* revealed the bunker's existence in 1992, and it was subsequently decommissioned. It has since been renovated and now houses a data storage facility for the private sector.

More than Trivia *Interesting Stories and Fascinating Facts*

Places

#288 Casey, Illinois, may be a small town (pop. 2,404), but there are many BIG things to see there, including several that landed them in the *Guinness World Records*. The first BIG thing built were wind chimes, the longest of the five chimes being 42 feet. There is also a 56.5-foot tall rocking chair, a giant mailbox, a 60-foot long pitchfork, a 26-foot tall key, and a 30-foot tall golf tee at the Casey Country Club. Not everything in Casey is the world's largest, but there are many more mighty big things to see there. *(https://www.bigthingssmalltown.com/)*

Chapter 7

Food

#289 A Mexican version of the fortune cookie is called the Lucky Taco. The red taco-shaped cookie also has a fortune inside.

#290 In an attempt to provide healthier food options for children, McDonald's once tried bubble gum-flavored broccoli. As you can imagine, it didn't go over well, and it didn't last long.

#291 In 2014, Taco Bell hired 25 men from across the country named Ronald McDonald to be in a commercial advertising Taco Bell's new breakfast menu. All the Ronalds were told to say, "I'm Ronald McDonald, and I love Taco Bell's new breakfast."

#292 Two universities have created a licking machine to determine how many licks it takes to get to the center of a Tootsie Roll Pop. The machine at Purdue University took 364 licks, and the one at the University of Michigan took 411 licks. Curious, though, because some student volunteers at Purdue only needed 252 licks.

Food

#293 Coffee was introduced into Turkey in the 15th century and became an essential part of its culture. At some point, a law was created that gave a woman the right to divorce her husband if he didn't provide her with the necessary amount of coffee. It can be said that insufficient coffee was the "grounds" for divorce.

#294 The Fossil Fuels Brewing Company was co-founded in 2008 by Microbiologist Raul Cano, who claims to have used yeast that is millions of years old. This yeast comes from revived microorganisms in fossilized tree resin known as amber, similar to the process used in the movie *Jurassic Park*. People who have tried his beer describe it as having a distinctive flavor.

#295 McDonald's Big Mac sandwich was created by one of McDonald's first franchisees Jim Delligatti and first served in 1967 in Uniontown, Pennsylvania. Forty miles away in Irwin, Pennsylvania, there is a Big Mac museum with a 14-foot-tall sculpture of the iconic sandwich. Before settling on Big Mac, he tried a few other names for the sandwich, such as the Aristocrat and the Blue Ribbon Burger.

#296 Many cultures have unique foods that are not widely known outside that culture. In Filipino culture, two such foods are "Banana ketchup" and "Liver spread." Banana ketchup is made using banana, sugar, vinegar, and spices and is often colored red to resemble tomato ketchup. It was first produced in large quantities in 1942 and is used as a condiment for fried chicken, hot dogs, hamburgers, omelets, spaghetti, and french fries. Liver spread is a pureed mixture of pork, beef, or chicken liver and cereal. It is similar to German liverwurst and is commonly eaten as a sandwich filling or a spread on crackers.

More than Trivia   *Interesting Stories and Fascinating Facts*

Food

#297 Sunflower seeds with a black husk are usually pressed to extract their oil. Striped sunflower seeds are primarily eaten as a snack food.

#298 Morton, Illinois, is called the "Pumpkin Capital of the World." It produces 85% of the world's canned pumpkins. They have an annual Pumpkin Festival that attracts over 75,000 people.

#299 Chicken soup has long been a form of folk medicine to treat common cold symptoms. It contains an amino acid similar to *acetylcysteine*, which doctors use for patients with bronchitis and other respiratory infections to help clear them up.

#300 Norway and Sweden have banned Skittles candy, not for the titanium dioxide it contains, but for the yellow 5 and yellow 6 coloring dyes in the candy. Though the EU said in 2021 that titanium dioxide in food is unsafe, they are more worried about allergic reactions and hyperactivity in children caused by the coloring dyes in Skittles and other foods.

#301 There is an annual American hot dog competitive eating competition called Nathan's Famous International Hot Dog Eating Contest. It is held each year on Independence Day at Nathan's restaurant in Coney Island, New York. The winner is the one that eats the most hot dogs and buns in ten minutes (and keeps them down). The winner of the competitive eating contest gets the coveted Mustard Belt. The record is 76 hot dogs in the 2021 men's division and 48.5 hot dogs in the 2020 women's division. ESPN has broadcast the contest for several years and has an agreement to broadcast the contest through 2024.

Interesting Stories and Fascinating Facts   **More** than Trivia

Food

#302 Cotton candy was invented by dentist William Morrison and candy maker John C. Wharton in 1897. Originally called "Fairy Floss," they sold 68,655 boxes at the 1904 World's Fair at 25 cents per box.

#303 The button-shaped candy we know as M&M's gets its name from the company's founders, Forrest Mars Sr. and Bruce Murrie. Mars is the son of Mars candy founder Frank Mars, and Murrie is the son of Hershey Chocolate's president William Murrie.

#304 George H.W. Bush, our 41st president, hated broccoli. He once said, "I do not like broccoli. And I haven't liked it since I was a little kid. And my mother made me eat it. Now I'm president of the United States. And I'm not gonna eat any more broccoli!" His wife, Barbara, did like broccoli. The United Fresh Fruit and Vegetable Association president once gave First Lady Barbara Bush a bouquet of broccoli and an additional 10 tons of the vegetable, which the White House donated to a local food bank. After Bush's comments, broccoli became more popular, and sales increased.

#305 The Meyer lemon is sweeter than the standard supermarket lemon. It is only slightly tart and tastes like a tangerine. It became popular in California in the 1970s and later when Martha Stewart began featuring them in recipes. It originated in China primarily as an ornamental tree. It was introduced in the U.S. by agricultural explorer Frank Meyer in 1908, who worked for the U.S. Department of Agriculture. Most of the Meyer lemon trees were destroyed in the mid-1940s when it was discovered that many had a citrus virus that killed millions of citrus trees worldwide. A new virus-free Meyer lemon tree was found in the 1950s and released in 1975 as the Improved Meyer lemon.

More than Trivia   *Interesting Stories and Fascinating Facts*

Food

#306 Sliced bread was first sold in 1928. In 1943, the U.S. imposed a short-lived ban against it as a wartime conservation measure. With much public outcry, the ban was rescinded after only 7 weeks.

#307 When Beatlemania broke out in 1963, fans of the Beatles in the U.S. pelted the band with jelly beans emulating fans in the UK who threw the British candy Jelly Babies at George Harrison, who reportedly liked eating them.

#308 The Domino's Pizza logo originally had three dots, representing the three stores in 1965 in the Ypsilanti, Michigan area. The owner, Tom Monaghan, planned to add a new dot with the addition of every new store. This idea soon became impractical as by 1978, the company had expanded to 200 stores. They opened their first international store in Manitoba, Canada, in 1983. By 2019, the company had grown to 10,000 international locations. Domino's Pizza of China offers American-style potato bacon pizza, crayfish crispy and tender chicken pizza, durian pulp pizza, salted egg yolk pizza, and Sichuan pepper flavor tender chicken drumsticks.

#309 Steve Henson, a plumbing contractor, created ranch dressing in the mid-1950s while working in Alaska. He moved to California in 1956, bought a dude ranch, and renamed it Hidden Valley Ranch. His Hidden Valley Ranch dressing was popular with the guests at his ranch. In 1957, he created a packaged mix of his dressing to sell in stores and later by mail for 75 cents each. He closed the dude ranch in the 1960s, but his mail-order business was doing so well that he had to open a factory to keep up with all the business. By this time, supermarkets nationwide carried his ranch dressing. In 1972, Clorox bought the Hidden Valley Ranch brand for $8 million, and Henson retired.

Interesting Stories and Fascinating Facts   **More** than **Trivia**

#310 According to The National Hot Dog and Sausage Council (NHDSC), Americans consume about 20 billion hot dogs yearly, including about 150 million on the 4th of July.

#311 Bustanica is the world's largest vertical farm, and it is in Dubai, UAE. The facility produces over 2 million pounds of leafy greens annually and uses 95% less water than a traditional farm.

#312 The first drive-thru at a McDonald's restaurant opened in 1975 in Sierra Vista, Arizona. It was created to accommodate local Fort Huachuca soldiers who were not allowed to wear their uniforms in public.

#313 Squashes, which are gourds, are one of the oldest known crops in the Americas. Virginia and New England settlers were not very impressed by the Indians' squash until they had to survive the harsh winter. At that point, they adopted squash and pumpkins as staples. Squashes were baked, cut, and moistened with animal fat, maple syrup, and honey.

#314 Vernors ginger ale is the oldest surviving ginger ale available. It was first served in 1880 by Detroit pharmacist James Vernor. When he first developed the formula, he included natural ginger to help with upset stomachs, drawing on the traditional use of ginger in Chinese medicine for gastrointestinal issues. Ginger is no longer listed as an ingredient in Vernors today. Vernors has had multiple owners throughout its history, including Pepsi-Cola, A&W, and Cadbury Schweppes, and is now owned by Keurig Dr Pepper. Singer Aretha Franklin had a Christmas ham glaze recipe that used Vernors ginger ale. Vernors released a black cherry flavor ginger soda in 2022, its first new flavor in over 50 years.

Food

#315 Though the grapefruit is much larger than a grape, there are two theories why it is called a grapefruit - 1. The premature grapefruit looks similar in shape to unripe green grapes, and 2. Grapefruits grow in clusters as a grape does, and they resemble the formation of large yellow grapes.

#316 At Zauo (Kanji for "sit" and "fish") Restaurant in Tokyo, Japan, you get to catch your dinner. You get a fishing pole and some bait when you walk in, and you sit on a giant boat surrounded by aquariums full of fish. You may see shark, red snapper, mackerel, and more. If it's in the water, you can try to catch it, and the cooks will prepare it for you. You can eat it raw, grilled, fried, steamed, or boiled.

#317 In 1919, at age 37, Roy W. Allen bought a root beer formula from a pharmacist in Arizona and began selling root beer at a roadside stand in Lodi, California. A year later, Allen partnered with Frank Wright, thus creating the A&W brand name. In 1924, Allen bought out Wright and began selling restaurant franchises. Allen retired in 1950 at the age of 68 and sold the business. In 1963, A&W became the first chain restaurant to serve a bacon cheeseburger. A&W also has a mascot called the Great Root Bear, or Rooty for short.

#318 German Chocolate Cake does not have German origin. It began in 1852 when American baker Samuel German developed dark baking chocolate for Baker's Chocolate Company. 105 years later, in 1957, Mrs. George Clay of Dallas, Texas, made a German Chocolate Cake with a recipe she created using German's Sweet Chocolate, which became very popular. Though not the original German Chocolate Cake, there is a popular chocolate cake with cherries that dates back to 1909 that is a favorite in Southern Germany, Austria, and Switzerland.

Interesting Stories and Fascinating Facts   **More** than Trivia

#319 Froot Loops (not Fruit Loops) is a Kellogg's cereal introduced in 1963. It has seven different colors, but each color tastes the same. They are all a fruit-flavored blend of apple, blueberry, cherry, lemon, lime, orange, and raspberry, but there is no fruit in the cereal.

#320 Jelly Belly jelly beans have been to outer space. They were a favorite of President Ronald Reagan, and he sent a plastic bag of them with the astronauts on the space shuttle *Challenger* in 1983 with a note on the bag saying, "Compliments of the White House." The astronauts had fun with them, tossing them into zero gravity and catching them in their mouths.

#321 The Margherita Pizza was invented in 1889 in Naples, Italy, in honor of the Queen of Italy, Margherita of Savoy. The toppings are tomato (red), mozzarella (white), and basil (green), ingredients inspired by the colors of the national flag of Italy. In Italy, it must be prepared in a certain way to be called a "pizza Margherita," and the Italian government certifies bakeries that make it correctly.

#322 The age-old question of whether a tomato is a fruit or a vegetable went to the Supreme Court in the 1893 case, *Nix v. Hedden*. This case arose because U.S. tax laws in the late 1800s charged a 10% tariff on imported vegetables but not on fruits. A New York company, John Nix & Co., imported fresh fruits and vegetables from various places worldwide. Nix tried to get out of paying the tax by arguing that tomatoes were technically fruits, not vegetables. The court ruled that from a Botanical point of view, tomatoes are the fruit of a vine, just as are cucumbers, squashes, beans, and peas. But in everyday language, they are all vegetables. So Mr. Nix had to pay the tax.

More than Trivia   *Interesting Stories and Fascinating Facts*

Food

#323 The Hawaiian pizza with pineapple and ham or bacon on a pizza was initially created by Sam Panopoulos in Ontario, Canada, in 1962. The pizza has nothing to do with the state of Hawaii but was named after the brand of canned pineapples they used at the time.

#324 Glen Bell initially operated a hog dog stand in 1948. But after seeing the popularity of the Mexican restaurant across the street, he learned how to make hard shell tacos and served them at his new stand in 1954 called Taco Tia. In 1962, he moved his restaurant to a 400-square-foot building in Downey, California, and called it Taco Bell, where he sold tostadas, burritos, frijoles, tacos, and more for 19 cents apiece.

#325 Tennessee brothers Barney and Ally Hartman invented Mountain Dew in the 1940s as a mixer to put in their whiskey. The term "Mountain Dew" was originally Southern slang for moonshine (homemade whiskey). Early marketing continued this imagery, including the cartoon character "Willie the Hillbilly." Pepsi-Cola acquired Mountain Dew in 1964 and changed the logo and marketing to reach a younger, outdoorsy generation.

#326 *Sommelier* is a term that used to apply only to experts of wine, but there is a growing popularity in the restaurant industry for water sommeliers. A water sommelier is a water expert trained to taste and evaluate water; some make recommendations for dining choices. Like wine has a *terroir* or region of origination that influences its taste, so does water. Most bottled water in America is treated tap water, whereas bottled water in Europe is primarily natural mineral water. The different minerals in water give it a unique taste. Some luxury bottled water, such as Lofoten Arctic Water, can cost over $50.

Interesting Stories and Fascinating Facts **More than Trivia**

Food

#327 The gummy bear was invented in 1922 by Hans Riegel, Sr., in Germany. He was inspired by the trained dancing bears seen at European street festivities during that time.

#328 There are over 100 official Jelly Belly jelly bean flavors, including Very Cherry, Buttered Popcorn, Caramel Corn, Cotton Candy, Orange Sherbet, Pomegranate, and Tutti-Frutti. They also have a BeanBoozled line of weird and wild flavors, including Booger, Dead Fish, Dirty Dishwater, Stink Bug, Barf, Rotten Egg, and Stinky Socks.

#329 McDonald's and Burger King have exclusive "Gold Cards" that give the holder free food, sometimes for life. McDonald's had a drawing in December 2022 where three winners got free food for life and an extra card to give away. Some famous people have the McGold Card, such as Bill Gates, Warren Buffet, and others. The Burger King gold card is quite exclusive as well. Jennifer Hudson got one as a former Burger King employee, and movie producer George Lucas also received one.

#330 The size of the salt crystal is the main difference between table salt and kosher salt. Table salt often has iodine added, a practice that began in the 1920s to combat iodine deficiencies. The larger crystals in kosher salt are flaky and coarse, making them excellent at drawing out moisture, including blood, from the meat. Eating blood is forbidden in some Jewish traditions, so the larger salt crystals of kosher salt are helpful for that. However, for something to be considered kosher, it must be manufactured under specific guidelines. So if you need real kosher salt, look for a package labeled "kosher certified." The two types of salt can be interchanged; just watch the quantities you use. Chefs generally prefer kosher salt over table salt.

More than Trivia *Interesting Stories and Fascinating Facts*

Food

#331 The Mr. Pibb soft drink was initially called Peppo. Coca-Cola, who owned Peppo, changed the name after Dr. Pepper sued them in 1972 for trademark infringement.

#332 Ruth Graves Wakefield and Sue Brides invented the chocolate chip cookie in 1938 when Wakefield owned Toll House Inn in Massachusetts. The original recipe is available online. (https://www.verybestbaking.com/toll-house/recipes/original-nestle-toll-house-chocolate-chip-cookies/)

#333 Depending on how you plan to use it, there is a right and wrong way to slice an onion. If you plan to use it raw, like in a salad or on a burger, it doesn't matter how you slice it. But if you want the onion pieces to maintain their shape even after cooking for a long time, you should slice them vertically, pole-to-pole.

#334 PEZ candy was first marketed in Vienna, Austria, in 1927. The name PEZ is an abbreviation of *PfeffErminZ* (German for peppermint). Though they are associated with the handheld PEZ candy dispenser, the original product was a round peppermint lozenge called PEZ drops packaged in round rolls. Over time, they were changed to the brick shape we know today and packaged in small metal tins. The popular handheld dispenser was invented and introduced at the Vienna Trade Fair in 1949. They began U.S. operations in 1952 and received their first U.S. patent that year for the dispenser. In 1957 they added a character head to the top of a dispenser. A Halloween Witch was the first character dispenser; a year later, Popeye was the first licensed character to be put on a dispenser. Today, there are over 550 unique dispenser heads with thousands of variations. Collecting the PEZ dispensers is very popular, and several annual conventions are held worldwide.

Interesting Stories and Fascinating Facts   **More** than **Trivia**

#335 *Byakuya* (Japanese for "white knight") is the world's most expensive ice cream at over $6,500 per serving as of May 2023. Developed by the Japanese gelato maker Cellato, the delicacy is made from a rare and expensive white truffle grown in Alba, Italy. It also has Parmigiano-Reggiano cheese, sake lees, and an edible gold leaf. The sake lees has a fruity taste and 8% alcohol.

#336 The Curtiss Candy Company renamed their Kandy Kake candy bar the Baby Ruth candy bar in 1921. Many thought this name change was because of the rising popularity of baseball slugger Babe Ruth. The company denied this claim and thus avoided paying royalties to the baseball star. They instead claim they named the candy after President Grover Cleveland's eldest daughter, Ruth Cleveland, who had died 17 years prior.

#337 Cheerios cereal came out in 1941 as "Cheerioats." The name was changed to "Cheerios" in December 1945 after Quaker Oats claimed to hold the rights to the term "oats." In addition to the original flavor, Cheerios produced about 30 other flavors through the years, including Honey Nut Cheerios (1979), Chocolate Cheerios (2010), Honey Vanilla Cheerios (2022), and a limited edition of Frosted Lemon Cheerios in 2023. Cheerios sold 139 million boxes of cereal in 2021.

#338 Each state in the U.S. has its favorite type of Christmas cookie. The nationwide leader is the Gingerbread cookie, picked by seven states, followed by the Italian Christmas cookie and the Peanut Butter Blossom cookie picked by six states each. Next is the Christmas Sugar cookie with five states. Four states each picked the Christmas Bar cookie and the Mexican Christmas cookie. Two states each picked the Candy Cane and Polish Christmas cookies. There were 14 other cookies selected chosen by one state each.

More than Trivia *Interesting Stories and Fascinating Facts*

Food

#339 In the 1950s, the Schweppes company created the term *schweppervescence* to describe its carbonated water's crisp, fizzy bubbles. People called the drink "lightning in a bottle."

#340 There is a Spam Museum in Austin, Minnesota, where you can learn about all things Spam. Spam was introduced by Hormel in 1937 to help the sales of pork shoulder, which did not sell well at that time. The meaning of the name Spam is known to only a small number of former Hormel Foods executives. Still, some have indicated that the name is a contraction of "spiced ham."

#341 *Pule* is the world's most expensive cheese at about $590 per pound. It is only made at the Zasavica Special Nature Reserve in Serbia. It is costly because it is difficult to produce, and one of its ingredients, the milk of a Balkan donkey, is rare and makes up 60% of the cheese. Only about 100 female Balkan donkeys are available to milk, and it takes 3 gallons of milk to make a pound of cheese. The Balkan donkey's milk is also used to make facial cream and soaps.

#342 Before the last McDonald's left Iceland in 2009, Hjortur Smarason bought one of the last McDonald's meals. Smarason didn't intend to eat it; he wanted to see if McDonald's food didn't decompose as he had heard. Three years later, he came across the hamburger and fries in the garage that he had put in a plastic bag, and there was no decomposition. So he donated the burger and fries to the National Museum of Iceland to be displayed for everyone to see. It was there for a year and now resides at the Snotra House hostel in southern Iceland. McDonald's put out a statement in 2020 claiming that their burgers don't seem to decompose due to a lack of moisture.

Interesting Stories and Fascinating Facts   **More** than Trivia

Food

#343 Both Kit Kat and Rolo chocolate candy are produced worldwide by Nestle, except in the United States, where the Hershey Company makes both.

#344 The most expensive, commercially available sandwich is the $214 "Quintessential Grilled Cheese" by Serendipity 3 in New York. It even has edible gold flakes.

#345 A peanut butter and banana sandwich is sometimes called "The Elvis" as it was a favorite of the King of Rock and Roll, and he sometimes had it with bacon on it.

#346 Stick candy has been around since the 1830s. It was the subject of an 1885 song, "The Candy Stick," a 1907 poem, "Stick-Candy Days," and a 1909 poem, "The Land of Candy."

#347 Mr. Jelly Belly, David Klein, created a new type of jelly bean in 1976, naming them after the blues musician Lead Belly. Today, it takes 7 to 14 days to make a Jelly Belly jelly bean. All beans are certified Kosher and gluten-free; each bean has four calories.

#348 Pepsi-Cola was initially called "Brad's Drink" after inventor Caleb Davis Bradham. Bradham had dropped out of medical school and became a public school teacher for a short time before opening a drug store in New Bern, North Carolina. Like many drug stores, it also had a soda fountain, and Bradham invented Pepsi-Cola there in 1893. The drink was advertised to relieve dyspepsia (indigestion) and had a cola flavor, hence Pepsi-Cola. Pepsi declared bankruptcy in 1923, and Coca-Cola had the chance to purchase it three times but declined. Pepsi later became more popular and recovered from its bankruptcy.

More than Trivia   *Interesting Stories and Fascinating Facts*

Food

#349 Animal crackers were given the name "Barnum's Animals" in 1902, featuring the circus theme of the Barnum and Bailey Circus. That same year, a box was designed for the Christmas season, complete with a string for hanging on the tree.

#350 Julius Pringles, aka Mr. P, has been the face of Pringles potato chips for over 30 years. Mr. P recently had a makeover, and some on social media pointed out that he resembles the Kidney Garden Spider. Pringles is now petitioning to have the Kidney Garden Spider renamed "The Pringles Spider." It remains to be seen if the American Arachnological Society will agree.

#351 Bangers and Mash is a classic British dish of sausages and mashed potatoes. It is commonly served with onion gravy and may also include English peas and fried onions. The sausages are called "bangers" because, during World War II, when there was a shortage of meat, they were made with a higher water content and would make a distinctive pop or bang sound when cooked.

#352 The inventor of Coca-Cola, John Pemberton, was a medical doctor and a Civil War Colonel. Wounded in the war and addicted to morphine, he wanted to find a substitute for morphine. When he launched Coca-Cola in 1886, two ingredients were cocaine (from the coca leaf) and caffeine (from the kola nut). Frank Mason Robinson, Pemberton's bookkeeper, created the Coca-Cola logo using a cursive script in a style of formal handwriting popular at that time. There was a conspiracy theory concerning the logo in Egypt in 1951. Some said it spelled out "No Mohammed, no Mecca" in Arabic when reflected in a mirror.

Interesting Stories and Fascinating Facts   **More** than Trivia

Food

#353 For pie, Pilgrims first hollowed out a pumpkin, filled it with apples, sugar, spices, and milk, then put the stem back on and baked it.

#354 Limes, being slightly more dense than lemons, will sink in water whereas lemons will float. It holds true whether the fruits are whole, peeled, or sliced.

#355 Though much of the chocolate consumed today is solid, the ancient Maya drank it. They mixed the paste from the ground cacao seeds with water, chili peppers, and other ingredients. If they sweetened it, they would use honey or flower nectar.

#356 The Tootsie Roll was America's first individually wrapped penny candy and has been made in the U.S. since 1907. Tootsie Roll founder Leo Hirschfield said the candy was named after his daughter Clara, whose nickname was "Tootsie." They were shipped overseas during World War II as part of the soldier's rations. Tootsie Roll's celebrity fans include Frank Sinatra, Sammy Davis Jr., and Jacqueline Kennedy Onassis.

#357 Pharmacist Charles Alderton created the Dr. Pepper soft drink around 1885 in Wade Morrison's Old Corner Drug Store in Waco, Texas. Alderton gave Morrison the formula, and Morrison named the drink Dr. Pepper, though it is unclear why. Some speculate that one of the drink's ingredients is a pepper extract and that associating Dr. with it gives the impression that it is a healthful drink. Another theory states it was named after one of two men in the Roanoke Valley area of North Carolina, where Morrison was from, who may have known Morrison - Dr. Charles T. Pepper or Dr. William Alexander Reed Pepper.

More than Trivia   *Interesting Stories and Fascinating Facts*

Food

#358 McDonald's Egg McMuffin was invented in 1972 to provide America with a drive-thru breakfast sandwich. It was originally served open-faced to resemble eggs Benedict and included a small tub of strawberry preserves on the side. The strawberry preserves didn't catch on, though you can still get them on request.

#359 Flavorists, also known as flavor chemists, utilize their knowledge of chemistry to develop both artificial and natural flavors. They typically have a background in chemistry, biology, or food science. The "Maillard reaction" is an example of how chemistry plays a role in food, as it produces the distinct flavor and effect of toasted bread or seared meat. In 1963, Pamela Low, a flavorist, came up with the original flavor for Cap'n Crunch cereal by drawing inspiration from her grandmother's brown sugar and butter recipe served over rice.

#360 Yams and sweet potatoes may look alike but are unrelated botanically. Africa grows over 600 varieties of yams, which make up 95% of the crop. When compared to sweet potatoes, yams are starchier and drier. Sweet potatoes come in two categories: firm and soft. When cooked, firm sweet potatoes remain firm, while soft sweet potatoes are moist and soft. In the United States, soft sweet potatoes are often incorrectly labeled as yams. This is because when soft sweet potatoes were first grown commercially, African slaves called them yams because they looked similar to those in Africa. The soft ones were marketed as yams to differentiate between the two types of sweet potatoes. Nowadays, the U.S. Department of Agriculture requires labels with the term yam to be accompanied by sweet potato. Unless you specifically search for yams, typically found in international markets, you are probably eating sweet potatoes.

Interesting Stories and Fascinating Facts **More** than **Trivia**

#361 Though tear-free onions called Sunions are available in some markets, most onions are so unpleasant to cut that you sometimes must stop and walk away for a minute or two before continuing. This is caused by chemical reactions when cutting into an onion. Without getting too technical, know that part of this involves sulfur-containing compounds. Yellow, purple, and white onions are the worst, and green onions aren't as bad. The less damage done to the onion, the better, so use a sharp knife to cut the onion.

#362 Necessity is the mother of invention, and that is how the fruit-flavored drink Fanta came into being. A trade embargo in World War II against Nazi Germany made it almost impossible to get Coca-Cola in Germany. Max Keith, head of Coca-Cola Germany, had the idea to create a new drink made of ingredients available in Germany, including sugar beet, whey, and apple pomace (leftover parts of an apple). Because of the strict sugar rationing, German citizens often used Fanta to sweeten soups and stews. The word "fantasy" inspired the brand name Fanta.

#363 As green and black tea leaves are from the same plant, *Camellia sinensis*, the difference between the types of tea depends on how the leaves are processed. The leaves are picked and immediately heated for green tea, typically by steaming, which prevents them from oxidizing, thus maintaining their green color. Leaves for black tea are picked, rolled, and crushed to aid in the oxidation process, which turns them from green to black. Black tea has almost twice as much caffeine as green tea (47 mg per 8 ounces for black versus 28 mg for green). But brewed coffee has about twice as much caffeine as black tea (96 mg per 8 ounces). Earl Grey tea is black tea with bergamot oil. Lady Grey tea (a registered trademark of Twinings) is black tea with bergamot oil, lemon peel, orange peel, and sometimes cornflower petals.

Food

#364 In 1884, Canadian pharmacist and chemist Marcellus Gilmore Edson was awarded a U.S. patent for making an early version of peanut butter called peanut paste.

#365 Some people love black licorice, and some people don't. Though Eastern medicine has used black licorice for thousands of years due to its many health benefits, it can cause health problems if eaten in large amounts. The FDA recommends that if you eat black licorice, do so in moderation and contact your healthcare provider if you have any health issues after eating it. Some candies contain anise oil, which tastes and smells like black licorice and doesn't have the potential risks.

#366 Ackee (*Blighia sapida*) is Jamaica's national fruit, but it is toxic if eaten before it is ripe and can even cause death. Unripe Ackee is green but turns a bright red, then yellow-orange as it ripens and splits open, revealing three shiny black seeds and a soft yellow flesh. Though it is a fruit, Ackee must be cooked before eating and is often combined with saltfish, onions, bell peppers, and tomatoes. Ackee and saltfish are Jamaica's national dish. The U.S. bans raw Ackee from being imported, but canned and frozen Ackee is available online and at some grocery stores.

#367 Everyone loves a cow that can't spell. Some fans teared up when Chick-fil-A restaurant announced in 2018 they would no longer publish their annual Cow Calendar. The popular calendars had a remarkable 20-year run with humorous illustrations of the "EAT MOR CHIKIN" writing cows. One person said the yearly calendar was "the highlight of my year." Fans were "shocked and hurt by the news," but they still love those tasty chicken sandwiches, and the restaurant has sat atop the list of fast food restaurants for customer satisfaction for the last eight years.

Interesting Stories and Fascinating Facts — **More** than **Trivia**

Chapter 8

Movies & TV

#368 Cookie Monster's real name is Sid. He is known for his voracious appetite for all cookies, but his favorite is chocolate chip. His signature song is "C is For Cookie."

#369 Dolph Lundgren, the actor who played Russian boxer Ivan Drago in the movie *Rocky IV*, has a master's degree in chemical engineering from the University of Sydney and was awarded a Fulbright scholarship to MIT. He is a world-class competitor in Japanese Karate and reportedly has an IQ of 160.

#370 E.T.'s favorite candy in the 1982 blockbuster movie was originally going to be M&M's. But Mars, maker of M&M's, declined, allowing second-choice Hershey's to step in with their Reese's Pieces as the treat that lured E.T. out of the bushes. Usually, a company has to pay to have its product featured in a film, but Hershey didn't. In exchange, they agreed to promote the movie with $1 million in advertising, and Hershey was allowed to use E.T. in their ads. Within two weeks after the film was released, sales of Reese's Pieces surged, and director Steven Spielberg had a new favorite candy.

Interesting Stories and Fascinating Facts **More** than Trivia

Movies & TV

#371 Dopey is the youngest of the seven dwarfs in *Snow White and the Seven Dwarfs* and the only one without a beard. Grumpy has the biggest nose of the seven. Happy is the only one with thick, white eyebrows (the others have thin black eyebrows like Walt Disney).

#372 The motion picture rating system has changed over the years. From 1972 to 1984, the ratings were G, PG, R, and X. During the 1980s, there were complaints about violence and gore in some films with a PG rating, so the PG-13 rating was introduced in 1984. The first film with the new PG-13 rating was *Red Dawn*, starring Patrick Swayze and Lea Thompson.

#373 *Mad Max, Fury Road*, was the fourth film in the Mad Max series by Australian filmmaker George Miller. Miller asked his wife, film editor Margaret Sixel, to edit the film though she had never edited an action film before. Miller felt that if edited by "the usual kind of guys, it would look like every other action movie we see." She had 470 hours of movie footage to edit, which took her about 2 years working 10 hours a day, six days a week. Sixel won the Academy Award for film editing in 2016 for her work on *Mad Max, Fury Road*.

#374 Toto, the Cairn Terrier in the 1939 film classic *The Wizard of Oz*, earned $125 per week during filming. The Munchkins earned $100 per week. Judy Garland, who played Dorothy, earned $500 per week. Bert Lahr (the Cowardly Lion) earned $2,500 per week, Ray Bolger (the Scarecrow) earned $3,000 per week, and Jack Haley (the Tin Man) also earned $3,000 per week. Buddy Ebsen, who played Jed Clampett on *The Beverly Hillbillies*, was the first choice for the Tin Man, but he was hospitalized after a bad reaction to the Tin Man's makeup. In 1974, Judy Garland's daughter Liza Minnelli married Jack Haley Jr., son of the Tin Man.

More than Trivia   *Interesting Stories and Fascinating Facts*

Movies & TV

#375 When making the 2019 live remake of the 1955 animated Disney movie *Lady and the Tramp*, the film crew searched nationwide for rescue dogs that looked like the on-screen animated characters. For Lady, they found an American Cocker Spaniel named Rose, a hunting dog from Texas. For Tramp, they found Monte, a Schnauzer/Shepherd mix, via an animal rescue group in Phoenix, Arizona. They both have new homes now with trainers from the movie. A big motivator treat used in their training was bacon.

#376 In the early 1900s, the movie industry relocated from the east coast to Hollywood to escape the strict control of Thomas Edison and the Motion Picture Patent Company (MPPC). Edison owned over 1,000 patents, including the Kinetoscope, a movie camera, and had a near monopoly over the industry. However, moviemakers found a solution in Hollywood's favorable weather and diverse scenery, which allowed them to create films without the interference of east coast patent holders. In 1915, a federal lawsuit ruled against the MPPC, and the organization ceased operations in 1918.

#377 *The Flintstones* animated sitcom was the first animated series on prime-time TV from 1960 to 1966. It was the most successful and longest-running network animated TV series for three decades until *The Simpsons* surpassed it in 1997. We all know about the Flintstones and the Rubbles, but there were other interesting families too. There was a stone age family of hillbillies called the "Hatrocks," including Granny and Jethro Hatrock. The Hatrocks didn't like "Bug" music like the "Four Insects," especially their song "She Said Yeah Yeah Yeah." Then there was the "Gruesome" family, the creepy but friendly family that moved in next door to the Flintstones. The Gruesome family featured Weirdly and Creepella Gruesome with their son "Gobby" Gruesome and Uncle Ghastly.

Interesting Stories and Fascinating Facts **More** than **Trivia**

Movies & TV

#378 Snake wranglers were hired for the 2014 film, *The Maze Runner*, to ensure the filming area was snake free. It's a good thing, as the wranglers found 25 venomous snakes, including a 5-foot-long rattlesnake.

#379 The first 3D movie was *The Power of Love* in 1922. With the 3D glasses, the audience could view one of two different endings, either a happy or a tragic ending. Another company later acquired the film and distributed it in 2D as *The Forbidden Lover* in 1923-24.

#380 James Cameron, the writer, and director of such successful films as *Avatar*, *Titanic*, *The Terminator*, and others, wasn't always the successful director he is today. He wanted to direct *The Terminator*, which he wrote in 1984, but his previous directing of *Piranha II: The Spawning* in 1981 was not well received. He subsequently sold the rights to *The Terminator* for $1 with the agreement that he would be the film's director, a decision he later regretted as the film has brought in over $78 million worldwide. Fortunately, because of copyright laws Cameron was due to get his rights back for *The Terminator* in 2019.

#381 Actor Bela Lugosi was best known for playing Count Dracula in the 1931 classic horror movie *Dracula*. When he died in 1956, he was buried wearing one of his Dracula capes and full costume. Interestingly, Universal Studios did not initially want Lugosi to be Dracula in the movie because he wasn't well known. However, he had previously played the lead role of Dracula in the popular New York stage version that ran for nine months. The studio changed its mind about Lugosi and paid him $3,500 to play the part. Because of the success of *Dracula*, Lugosi was offered to play the role of Frankenstein but did not want to be typecast as a horror actor, and he felt the makeup would cover up his good looks.

More than Trivia   *Interesting Stories and Fascinating Facts*

Movies & TV

#382 Filmmaker George A. Romero has been called the "Father of the Zombie Film" after his *Night of the Living Dead* series of films and other zombie films. But one of his early commercial films was a segment for *Mister Rogers' Neighborhood* in which Fred Rogers underwent a tonsillectomy.

#383 Actor Jim Caviezel who portrayed Jesus Christ in the movie *The Passion of the Christ*, was struck by lightning during the filming. He survived the incident, but it terrified him. Incidentally, Caviezel was 33 years old when he played the part of Jesus, the same age as Jesus was when he died. Caviezel also has the same initials – J.C.

#384 In the 1971 movie *Diamonds Are Forever*, Clint Eastwood, Burt Reynolds, and Adam West declined the offer to play James Bond because they believed that a British actor should portray the character. For the James Bond role in *Dr. No*, Cary Grant felt he was too old, Patrick McGoohan felt the role was too promiscuous, and Rod Taylor felt the part was beneath him.

#385 Actress Lauren Bacall, born Betty Joan Perske, began her career as a model appearing on the magazine covers of *Vogue* and *Harper's Bazaar*. At age 17, she took acting classes, where she dated classmate Kirk Douglas. Early in her career, she took voice lessons to change her natural high-pitched, nasal voice to the low, husky voice for which she was known. She had to shout verses from Shakespeare daily for hours as part of her voice training. At 5 feet, 8 1/2 inches, she was taller than most actresses at the time except for Swedish actress Ingrid Bergman, who was 5 feet, 9 inches tall. Incidentally, Bergman was 2 inches taller than her Casablanca co-star Humphrey Bogart, who was also Bacall's husband.

Interesting Stories and Fascinating Facts **More** than **Trivia**

Movies & TV

#386 Disney's 1937 film *Snow White and the Seven Dwarfs* is the first American film to have a soundtrack album released with the film. Some of the more well-known songs written for the film include "Someday My Prince Will Come," "Whistle While You Work," and "Heigh-Ho."

#387 Actress Lucille Ball and her husband, Desi Arnaz, owned Hollywood's Desilu Productions, which became one of the largest independent production companies. After their divorce, Lucy bought out Desi's share in 1962, making her one of the most influential women in Hollywood. She had a keen eye for successful TV shows and financed the first *Star Trek* pilot, "The Cage," which unfortunately failed. However, she funded a second pilot, "Where No Man Has Gone Before," which included Mr. Spock from the first pilot and new cast members William Shatner (Captain Kirk), George Takei (Sulu), and James Doohan (Scottie). The show became a hit and is the well-known *Star Trek* series we know today.

#388 Though very successful as an actor, Clint Eastwood originally wanted to pursue a music career. That didn't work out how he wanted, but he does now have his own Warner Bros. Records imprint called Malpaso Records. His record company has released all the scores of his films since *The Bridges of Madison County*. He has composed the film scores of seven of his movies and the original piano composition for *In the Line of Fire*. Eastwood wrote and performed the song heard over the credits of *Gran Torino*. The title song in *Grace is Gone*, with music by Eastwood and lyrics by Carole Bayer Sager, was nominated for Best Original Song. In 2007, he was awarded an honorary Doctor of Music degree from the Berklee College of Music at the Monterey Jazz Festival, where he is an active board member.

More than Trivia   *Interesting Stories and Fascinating Facts*

Movies & TV

#389 Sylvester Stallone wanted his *Rocky IV* boxing scenes to look authentic, so he told Dolph Lundgren, his boxing opponent in the movie, to "Just go out there and try to clock me." Lundgren followed orders, and Stallone wound up in the hospital for nine days when Lundgren connected with an uppercut to Stallone's ribs.

#390 *Plan 9 From Outer Space* has been called, by many, the worst film ever made. In the *Seinfeld* episode "The Chinese Restaurant," Jerry and his friends try to get a dinner table before seeing *Plan 9* for its one-night showing. In a 2000 *The X-Files* episode called "Hollywood A.D.," Agent Scully visits Fox Mulder at his home where he is watching *Plan 9* and comments he has seen it 42 times. The original title was *Grave Robbers from Outer Space* but later changed to *Plan 9 From Outer Space*. The film is an independent sci-fi horror film shot in black and white in 1956, released in 1959, and sold to TV in 1961. It is the last film that Bela Lugosi appeared in. It is such a well-known terrible movie that it has gained a cult following.

Interesting Stories and Fascinating Facts **More** than **Trivia**

Movies & TV

More than Trivia *Interesting Stories and Fascinating Facts*

Chapter 9

Celebrations

#391 The Boryeong Mud Festival has been held yearly in Boryeong, South Korea, since 1998. It is called the largest summer festival in the world and attracts millions of visitors each year. The mud from the Boryeong mud flats is rich in minerals and used to make cosmetics. The festival lasts ten days and includes mud slides, mud prison, mud skiing, and a mud pool.

#392 The small city of Dinant, Belgium (pop. 13,544), is the birthplace of Adolphe Sax, inventor of the saxophone, and it is the location of *La Regate des Baignoires*, an annual bathtub race on the Meuse River. The one-kilometer (.6 miles) race has occurred annually on August 15 since 1982, and the event is free for participants and attendees. Competitors often decorate their crafts creatively and in ways that enhance their floating abilities. The bathtubs must be self-propelled with no motors allowed, and any number of people can be on a single vessel. About 50 teams compete yearly, and the event often draws up to 25,000 people.

Interesting Stories and Fascinating Facts   **More** than **Trivia**

Celebrations

#393 The city of Pacific Grove, California, has a Butterfly Parade each October to celebrate the return of the monarch butterfly to the area for the winter. They also have a city ordinance that makes killing or threatening a butterfly a misdemeanor crime, with a $1,000 fine.

#394 In 1924, the initial Macy's Thanksgiving Day Parade was held with store employees who wore colorful outfits. The parade included floats, professional bands, and live animals from the Central Park Zoo. At the 34th Street store entrance, Santa Claus appeared on Macy's balcony and was named "King of the Kiddies." This event attracted an audience of more than 250,000 people.

#395 There are two National Doughnut Days to celebrate each year in the U.S. The holiday on the first Friday of June of each year honors the ladies of the Salvation Army who served doughnuts to soldiers during World War I. The second doughnut holiday is on November 5, celebrating that sweet ring of delicious dough. One of the earliest descriptions of a doughnut is Washington Irving's 1809 *History of New York* where he mentions balls of sweetened dough fried in hog fat that he called donuts. We know these today as doughnut holes.

#396 Brown Friday is the busiest day of the year for plumbers, but not necessarily for the reason you think. Brown Friday is the day after Thanksgiving when a lot of food is served, and a lot of food waste goes down the sink that shouldn't. Thus, there are a lot of clogged drains and jammed garbage disposals on Turkey Day and the day after. So be smart about what you put down the drain. Some things that should not go down the drain are grease, potato peels, bones, cornhusks, onion skins, carrot peelings, fibrous vegetables, coffee grounds, and egg shells.

More than Trivia   *Interesting Stories and Fascinating Facts*

Celebrations

#397 Each November, people from all over Japan visit the village of Kushihara, Japan, to buy and eat wasp delicacies. One of the most popular is *hachinoko gohan*, which is wasp larvae with steamed rice. There is also a wasp-cultivating competition where the person with the heaviest wasp nest is the winner.

#398 For 2,000 years, dragon boat racing has been a popular sport in China. The boats typically have a crew of 18-20 who paddle while facing forward, similar to canoeing. In competitive events, the boats are equipped with Chinese dragon heads. The International Dragon Boat Federation (IDBF) oversees the sport worldwide. The Dragon Boat Festival was created to honor Chinese poet Qu Yuan, who was accused of treason, exiled, and ultimately drowned himself in the Miluo River. Locals tried to save him or retrieve his body by racing out in boats. When they couldn't find him, they dropped sticky rice balls in the water to prevent fish from eating his body.

#399 The *Eukonkanto*, or Wife-Carrying contest, originated in Finland. These contests have taken place in many parts of the world. Still, the Wife Carrying World Championships have been held annually in Sonkajärvi, Finland, since 1992, where the prize is the wife's weight in beer. Several types of carrying may be practiced: a classic piggyback, a fireman's carry (over the shoulder), or Estonian-style (wife upside-down on his back with her legs over the neck and shoulders). The length of the official track is 832 feet, and the minimum weight of the woman being carried is 108 pounds. The wife to be carried may be your own or the neighbor's, or you may have found her further afield; she must be over 17 years of age. There are several other rules for the contest, but one of the most important ones is "All participants must enjoy themselves."

Interesting Stories and Fascinating Facts **More** than **Trivia**

Celebrations

#400   A unique Christmas tradition is that of the "Christmas pickle." The Christmas pickle is a decoration hidden on the Christmas tree, and whoever finds it supposedly has good fortune during the following year. Berrien Springs, Michigan (pop. 1,800), was known as the Christmas pickle capital of the world for many years, having parades, activities, and a Pickle Prince and Princess contest.

#401   The World Toe Wrestling Championship has been held annually since 1994 in Derbyshire, UK. It is not a soft sport; competitors sometimes break one or more toes during a contest. One of the sport's most dominating players was 64-year-old Alan "Nasty" Nash, undefeated for 17 years before losing to 34-year-old Ben Woodroffe in 2022. On the women's side, Lisa "Twinkletoes" Shenton was a previous world champion, but Dawn Millward is the current champion.

#402   Cooper's Hill is a well-known landmark that hosts an annual cheese rolling contest in the small village of Brockworth, located in southwest Britain. This event, known as "the world's most dangerous footrace," involves participants chasing a 7-9 pound roll of Double Gloucester cheese down a steep 200-yard hill. The cheese is given a one-second head start and can reach 70 mph. While everyone starts running, many end up rolling and tumbling down the hill. Due to liability issues, the contest has been an unmanaged and spontaneous event since 2010. It is common for ambulances to be present at the bottom of the hill due to the inevitable injuries. Luckily, local rugby team members and the Young Farmers Club are on hand to assist those who need help. The event includes multiple contests throughout the day, with separate events for men and women. The winner receives the coveted cheese prize. This popular contest is said to be more than 600 years old.

More than **Trivia**   *Interesting Stories and Fascinating Facts*

Celebrations

#403 The 2022 national average cost of running Christmas lights from Thanksgiving to New Year's Day is $16.48. The most expensive state is Hawaii at $38.46, and the least costly is Washington at $10.51.

#404 *Escargot* (edible snail) is a favorite of French cuisine. There are festivals every year in different parts of France for people to gather and enjoy the delicacy. One of the larger festivals is the *Aplec del Cargol* (snail gathering) in northeast France, where 200,000 people gather yearly. One of the favorites at the festival is *Cargols a la Llauna*. It is made with a combination of snails, mayonnaise, and garlic.

#405 Many people in the U.S. cherish a white Christmas, but with an average temperature of 69 degrees and little chance of snow, West Palm Beach, Florida, celebrates the holiday season with the "Sandi Tree." This tradition started in 2012 and features a 35-foot, 700-ton Christmas tree sand sculpture in downtown West Palm Beach. The festivities commence with the lighting of the tree in early December and continue throughout the month with musical performances, nightly light shows, and numerous other activities.

#406 For more than 400 years, Japan has celebrated the *Naki Sumo* Crying Baby Festival. During the festival, parents bring their babies to be held by Sumo wrestlers, who compete against each other to make the baby cry first or the loudest. To achieve this, the Sumo wrestlers make faces, loud noises, or shout, "Cry, Cry, Cry" at the baby. The winning baby receives a blessing of good health. This tradition has its roots in two beliefs; one is a proverb that says, "Crying babies grow fat," and the other is that crying wards off evil spirits. The festival is so popular that parents from all over Japan travel to participate.

Interesting Stories and Fascinating Facts   **More** than **Trivia**

Celebrations

#407 The World's Largest Brat Fest is held each Memorial Day weekend in Madison, Wisconsin. Since 1983, Brat Fest has sold more than 4 million brats, raising almost $2 million for local charities.

#408 The average Christmas tree purchased from a tree farm takes up to 10 years to grow to six feet tall. Across the United States, approximately 15,000 tree farms cultivate around 350 million Christmas trees. However, the majority of these trees come from Oregon and North Carolina. Every year, about 25-30 million trees are harvested.

#409 An underwater music festival is held yearly near Big Pine Key, Florida, to raise awareness for coral preservation. Music is streamed from underwater speakers and broadcast live on a local FM radio station. Musician divers and mermaids play instruments such as the "trom-bonefish," "bass-oon," and "manta-lin." There are always ocean-themed songs, such as the Beatles' "Yellow Submarine," or the *Gilligan's Island* theme song. There are also reef rockstar performers such as "Paul McCarpney" and "Ringo Starfish."

#410 The International Hair Freezing Contest, held at the Eclipse Nordic Hot Springs in Yukon, Canada, began in 2011. There are five competition categories, with each winner getting $2,000 CAN (~$1,500 USD). The contest begins in February when the outside temperature reaches -4 degrees Fahrenheit and ends on March 25, 2023. There were 288 entries in 2020. To enter, you must dip your head in the hot springs to get your hair completely wet. Then raise your head out of the water and let your hair slowly freeze (so will your eyebrows and eyelashes). Once your hair has lots of frost and ice buildup and is shaped to your liking, you ring a bell for a staff member to come out and take your picture.

More than Trivia   *Interesting Stories and Fascinating Facts*

Celebrations

#411 Though Festivus was made popular on the TV show *Seinfeld*, it was conceived by author Daniel O'Keefe and celebrated as early as 1966. If you don't have one, start your own quirky holiday tradition.

#412 The annual Pasadena Chalk Festival began in 1993 as "Chalk It Up" and featured 150 chalk artists participating. In 2010, it attracted over 600 artists and 100,000 visitors and used over 25,000 chalk sticks in one weekend. That year it was officially named the Largest Display of Chalk Pavement Art by *Guinness World Records*. It is free to the public. Check out their website (www.pasadenachalkfestival.org) for more info and examples of the artwork.

#413 Images of Santa Claus in America usually include snow and reindeer, but it's not that way in other parts of the world. Santa has arrived on Christmas Eve at a beach in Mooloolaba, a Queensland, Australia coastal town for the last sixty years, wearing sunglasses. Though he typically arrives by surf boat, he parasailed to the area for some years, and his reindeer (lifeguards with antlers), would pick him up in a rescue boat and row him to shore. About 2,000 families visit the beach on Christmas Eve to see Santa's arrival.

#414 The Highland Games occur annually in Scotland and other parts of the world, celebrating Scottish and Celtic culture. The event features several athletic competitions, such as the Stone Put, Weight over the Bar, and the Sheaf Toss, as well as plenty of dancing and music. A highlight for many spectators is watching 20 or more pipe bands march together and play popular tunes like "Scotland the Brave" or "Amazing Grace." The biggest Highland Games celebration is the Braemar Gathering, held every September, attended by the reigning monarch and members of the Royal Family since 1348.

Interesting Stories and Fascinating Facts **More than Trivia**

Celebrations

#415 The Golden Retriever Festival, aka Guisachan Gathering, is held yearly at the former Guisachan mansion in the Scottish Highlands. Guisachan is where Lord Tweedmouth originally bred golden retrievers in 1868. The first litter had four puppies: Ada, Cowslip, Crocus, and Primrose. The event is typically held in July and features activities, food, and hundreds of golden retrievers competing for prizes. See more info at https://friendsofguisachan.org/.

#416 In the Republic of Georgia, formerly part of the Soviet Union, it is customary to dine with the deceased in graveyards during Easter time each year. The meal served typically includes wine, a sweet bread known as paska, and red-dyed eggs to signify Christ's sacrifice and resurrection, made using madder root or onion skin. Some families go all out and bring a complete feast with a table. The purpose of this tradition is to remember and pay tribute to loved ones who have passed away. It also symbolizes the start of spring signifying that death is not the end and new life begins.

#417 For over 120 years, Oaxaca, Mexico, has had a radish carving competition called "Night of the Radishes." These radishes differ from the typical grocery store radish. These are heavily fertilized, chemically treated, and left in the ground for a long time to become large, misshapen radishes. They can measure up to 20" x 4" and weigh 6+ pounds. The radishes are not suitable for eating and will quickly start to wilt so the competition only lasts a few hours. There are generally over a hundred participants and thousands of visitors. There are several competition categories, but the traditional category has a grand price of 15,000 pesos (~$900). As the competition is held each year on December 23, many of the entries are Nativity themed, but there are also Oaxacan traditions depicted and others. Wait times to see all entries can take 4 or 5 hours.

More than Trivia   *Interesting Stories and Fascinating Facts*

Chapter 10

Curiosities

#418   Two people are crushed to death every year in the United States by trying to tilt faulty vending machines.

#419   In 2008, two sisters from Virginia sold their Illinois-shaped corn flake on eBay for $1,350 to an owner of a trivia website. Shortly after that auction, other state-shaped food items appeared on eBay.

#420   Delta Dental reported that in 2021, the average amount given by Tooth Fairies in the U.S. for a child's tooth was $4.70. However, Tooth Fairies in the Northeast were more generous, giving an average of $5.72 per tooth, while those in the Midwest gave an average of $3.66.

#421   A rude type of valentine's card called the "Vinegar Valentine" was sent anonymously in the Victorian era to insult someone or let them know their affection or attention was unwanted. And what made it worse was that the recipient had to pay the postage on the card. They usually contained an insulting poem and illustration.

Curiosities

#422 The Birkenstock sandals that Steve Jobs wore in the 1970s and 1980s sold at an auction for $218,750 in November 2022. He wore the Birkenstocks when he and Steve Wozniak created Apple Computer from a Los Altos, California garage.

#423 9 of the 10 most common birthdays are in September (9th, 19th, 12th, 17th, 10th, 20th, 15th, 16th, and 18th, respectively). July 7 is #6 on the list. The least common births occur on a holiday or the day after. Part of the reason for fewer births around holidays is that fewer C-sections are scheduled then.

#424 Sometimes, fortune cookies have a string of numbers on the paper that contains the fortune. In 2005, a Powerball lottery drawing had 110 second-place winners attributing their success to the numbers they found in a fortune cookie. 89 people won $100,000 with the fortune cookie number, and 21 won $500,000 because they chose the Power Play multiplier option. Lottery officials investigated the unusually high number of second-place winners and found no foul play, only good fortunes.

#425 Thanks to Robert Thomas, a fish and wildlife technician from New York, we now have an answer to the age-old question: "How much wood would a woodchuck chuck if a woodchuck could chuck wood?" In 1988, Thomas measured the volume of dirt in a typical 35-square-foot woodchuck burrow and determined that if the woodchuck could move the equivalent volume of wood, it could "chuck" approximately 700 pounds of it. However, it's important to note that woodchucks can't actually chuck wood - the term woodchuck actually originated from the Native American name *wuchak*, which later evolved into woodchuck.

More than **Trivia**   *Interesting Stories and Fascinating Facts*

Curiosities

#426 Map making is a fascinating subject with over two thousand years of history. One of the more intriguing maps ever made was the *Tabula Rogeriana* by cartographer Muhammad al-Idrisi in 1154 at the request of Sicily's King Roger II. His work took 15 years to complete and comprised a book with 70 sectional maps and a 300 lb. silver disk over 6 feet across engraved with a world map based on his sectional maps. Amazingly, his work estimated the earth's circumference to be 22,900 miles when we now know it is 24,901 miles, a difference of less than 10%.

#427 On January 1, 1913, when the U.S. Postal Service started delivering packages weighing more than 4 pounds, many weird things were put in the mail. One Ohio couple mailed their baby boy to his grandmother's house about a mile away. They paid 15 cents for the stamps and enough to insure him for $50 and handed him over to the mailman who dropped off the boy at nana's house. After this was done by other parents in 1913 and 1914, the Postal Service decided that sending people through the mail was no longer acceptable. Then in 1920, sending people through the mail became a federal crime.

#428 A white oak tree in Athens, Georgia, legally owns itself. Even though a tree is not a legal person and can neither deed nor own property itself, the position of the Athens-Clarke County Unified Government is that the tree, despite the law, does indeed own itself. If the truth is told, the current tree is actually the "Son of The Tree That Owns Itself." The original tree was "Deeded to Itself" sometime around 1830 and developed root rot and fell over in late 1942. The lot the tree was on was vacant for four years after its demise. Several residents had grown a new tree from acorns of the original tree, and one of the best specimens was planted and dedicated in December 1946. The tree is now over 50 feet tall and was locally designated a historic landmark on February 2, 1988.

Interesting Stories and Fascinating Facts **More than Trivia**

Curiosities

#429 Horseshoes have long been considered lucky. Superstitious sailors believe nailing a horseshoe to the mast will help their vessel avoid storms. Some nail a horseshoe above the door to their home with the open side pointing down to represent the luck poured upon those who enter.

#430 As part of Melbourne, Australia's 2012-2032 Urban Forest Strategy, the city assigned email addresses to all of their 77,000 trees so that residents could report trees that had been damaged or that needed extra care. They did not expect to receive over 3,000 emails worldwide expressing love for the trees in Melbourne. Many letters shared thoughts and feelings about life as though the tree were a pen pal in a faraway land.

#431 The world's tallest average population is the Dinaric Alps in southern Europe. The average male is 6 ft 1 in tall, and the average woman is 5 ft 7 1/2 in tall. The populations of Bosnia/Herzegovina and the Netherlands are very close behind. The world's shortest average population is in East Timor in Southeast Asia. The average male is 5 ft 2 1/2 in tall, and the average woman is 5 ft 0 in tall. The populations of Guatemala, Liberia, Papua New Guinea, Nepal, and Cambodia are very close behind.

#432 A safety coffin is a coffin designed to allow a person to signal to the above-ground world that they are still alive. These were popular in the 19th century during the cholera epidemic, and several designs were patented during the 18th and 19th centuries. The alarm method was typically an external bell attached to a cord in the coffin. The term "saved by the bell" does not refer to the safety coffin alarm but is a boxing reference where a contestant is saved from a knockout or countdown by the ring of a bell, which signals the end of the round before they are counted out.

More than **Trivia**   *Interesting Stories and Fascinating Facts*

Curiosities

#433 Over 1,000 red-winged blackbirds fell from the sky dead on New Year's Eve, 2010, in Beebe, AR. State officials said the cause may have been weather related.

#434 A 2017 Innovation Center for U.S. Dairy survey showed that 7% of American adults think chocolate milk comes from brown cows. 7% doesn't sound like much, but that's about 16 million people. And 48% of adults weren't sure where chocolate milk comes from.

#435 Usually, the honey that bees make is an amber color. But in northeastern France in 2012, bees made some honey in shades of blue and green. As it turned out, the bees had consumed waste from a nearby biogas plant that was processing waste from a nearby chocolate factory that made M&M candy.

#436 The largest denomination of American paper currency currently printed is the $100 bill. The U.S. previously issued bills in larger denominations, such as $500, $1,000, $5,000, and $10,000. These larger bills are still legal tender and may still be in circulation. All U.S. currency issued since 1861 is valid and redeemable at its full face value.

#437 Almost 5 million Lego pieces were dumped into the ocean when a rogue wave hit the container ship *Tokio Express* about 20 miles off the southwest coast of Britain on February 13, 1997. In all, 62 containers were knocked overboard by the wave. The ship was en route to New York City, and many of the Legos were to go in toy kits featuring sea adventures. The residents of Cornwall County have been finding some of the Lego pieces washed up on shore since the accident.

Interesting Stories and Fascinating Facts   **More** than **Trivia**

Curiosities

#438 The Eagle Pencil Company made pencils for Thomas Edison to a particular specification. Each pencil was three inches long and thicker than standard pencils, and each had softer graphite than was generally used or available.

#439 In the 1980s, A & W Restaurant introduced a 1/3 pound burger priced the same as their competitor's smaller quarter pounder. However, sales were disappointing. A market research firm was subsequently hired to investigate the issue, and their findings were surprising. Many participants believed that a 1/4 pound burger contained more meat than a 1/3 pound burger and, thus, saw no reason to pay the same price for a smaller burger.

#440 A **micromort** is a risk level measurement that defines the mortality risk of various activities. One micromort is defined as a one-in-a-million chance of death. These are estimations based on past deaths for the particular activity. Some examples are Skydiving - 8 micromorts per jump; Scuba diving - 5 per dive; Hang gliding - 8 per jump; Heroin one-time use - 30; Going for a swim - 12; Getting out of bed (age 45) - 6; Being born - 430.

#441 After 87 years, Oscar Mayer's "Wienermobile" has a new name. It is now called the "Frankmobile" in honor of their new all-beef franks. Oscar Mayer has a fleet of six Frankmobiles nationwide, and drivers are now called "Frankfurters" instead of "Hotdoggers." College seniors about to graduate are eligible for the one-year assignment as a Frankfurter, and there are two Frankfurters aboard each Frankmobile. There are only 12 chosen each year for this coveted position out of the thousands (7,000 in 2018) that apply. You can track the Frankmobile "Meat Fleet" location on their website at https://www.oscarmayer.com/frankmobile.

More than Trivia   *Interesting Stories and Fascinating Facts*

Curiosities

#442 In 2022, a denim archaeologist found a pair of Levi's jeans from the 1880s in an abandoned mine. The jeans were in reasonably good condition and were sold at an auction for $87,400.

#443 In 2005, GoldenPalace.com paid $1,209 for a Nacho Cheese Doritos chip at an eBay auction that looks like the Pope's Mitre (the tall hat the Pope wears). The eBay page for the Doritos chip had over 41,000 visitors and 34 bids before GoldenPalace scooped it up.

#444 A 1974 survey of Icelanders born between 1904 and 1944 showed that 7% of them were sure of the existence of Elves (*Huldufólk* or Hidden People), and 45% claim it is likely or possible. Visitors to the Icelandic Elf School in Reykjavik can take a 5-hour excursion to learn about Icelandic folklore. Hafnarfjorour has a 90-minute "Hidden Worlds tour" through Hellisgerdi Park, said to be the town's largest elf colony. There is an Icelandic wonders museum in Stokkseyri where you can walk into a world of elves and get a glimpse of their life.

#445 In 2019, the Roosevelt Hotel in New Orleans celebrated its 125th anniversary by offering a prize worth $15,000 to the person who returned the most outrageous item ever stolen (borrowed?) from the hotel. They won't ask questions or contact the police and will even return the stolen item to you if you want. The winner received seven nights in the Presidential Suite (worth $1,500+ per night), free private dinners cooked by the executive chef, and spa treatments. More than 70 items were returned, including Grunewald plates, bud vases, giant brass room keys, a silver candelabra, and much more. The contest winner was Leigh Guglielmo of New Orleans, who returned a historic coffee pot.

Interesting Stories and Fascinating Facts **More** than **Trivia**

Curiosities

#446 About 10% of the world's population is left-handed, and men are more likely to be left-handed than women. Left-handed people typically have a higher intelligence in language and are above-average high achievers. Famous left-handers include Leonardo da Vinci, Nikola Tesla, Bill Gates, Steve Jobs, Paul McCartney, Jimi Hendrix, Beethoven, Mozart, Marilyn Monroe, Aristotle, Einstein, Marie Curie, and Mark Twain.

#447 **Hammerspace** is that fictional storage space in cartoons, video games, etc., where characters can pull an unlimited number or size of objects out of a bag or article of clothing, etc., where it is physically impossible or improbable to do so. Did you ever see the *Tom & Jerry* cartoon, where Jerry would pull a bat or mallet out of thin air and hit Tom with it? Curly on *The Three Stooges* would often have various tools or other items in his jacket. Hammerspace is not precisely the same as a Magic Bag like Santa had or like a plot hole on the *Highlander* TV series where no matter what he was wearing, Duncan McLeod could always pull a sword out of his clothing.

#448 The Sourtoe Cocktail is a traditional drink served to those who wish to become members of the Sourtoe Cocktail Club in Dawson City, Yukon. This unique drink typically consists of whiskey with a dehydrated and salt-preserved human toe added to it. The origin of the toe dates back to the 1920s when Louie Linken suffered from frostbite and had his toe amputated and preserved in alcohol by his brother Otto. In 1973, Dawson resident Captain Dick Stevenson discovered the jar containing the toe and suggested incorporating it into a drink. To become a member of the Sourtoe Cocktail Club, one must make contact with the toe with their lips while consuming the cocktail. The original toe only lasted seven years until someone accidentally swallowed it. Since then, other amputated toes have been donated, and the fine for swallowing one is $2,500.

More than Trivia *Interesting Stories and Fascinating Facts*

Curiosities

#449 In May 2023, Jim Perry returned a book titled *A Family History of the United States* to the Saint Helena Library in California. Jim found the book in a box of books belonging to his recently deceased wife. What was interesting about this book was that it was 96 years overdue. Jim's grandfather-in-law initially checked out the book in 1927. Luckily, Jim did not have to pay late fees as the library stopped collecting them in 2019.

#450 In December 2017, Swedish company IKEA ran an ad in a Swedish women's magazine called *Amelia* that asked women to pee on a specific area of the ad. If you were pregnant, the ad's offer would change, giving you a better price. IKEA is known for its creative marketing, and it felt this unique pregnancy test was a novel way to make people think of IKEA when considering having kids. Though some viewed the ad as bizarre, its overall response was favorable.

#451 The Barkley Marathon is known for being one of the world's most demanding and unique ultramarathons. It is held annually in Frozen Head State Park, Tennessee, with only 40 participants allowed. The runners have a strict time limit of 60 hours to complete the 100-mile course, which entails running a 20+ mile off-course trail five times, clockwise and counter-clockwise, with over 50,000 feet of accumulated vertical climb. Registration for the race fills up fast, and potential entrants must submit an essay on "Why I Should be Allowed to Run in the Barkley," pay a $1.60 application fee and fulfill other criteria, which may change over time. First-time runners must also bring a license plate from their state or country as part of the entrance fee. The race start time remains a mystery, with runners receiving a one-hour notice between midnight and noon on race day. Although three runners completed the 2023 race, there have been many years without any finishers.

Interesting Stories and Fascinating Facts **More** than Trivia

Curiosities

#452 In the late 1800s, you could buy divorce papers from a vending machine in Corinne, Utah, for $2.50 in coins.

#453 There are more than 5.5 million vending machines in Japan. They have the highest ratio of vending machines in the world, with one machine for every 23 people.

#454 Each bill of U.S. currency is 6.14 inches long, 2.61 inches wide, and .0043 inches thick. One strap of currency contains 100 bills and is .43 inches thick. One bundle contains 10 straps. One million dollars is 100 straps of one-hundred-dollar bills (10,000 bills). The color of the strap indicates the denomination of the bill. $1=blue, $2=green, $5=Red, $10=yellow, $20=violet, $50=brown, $100=mustard.

#455 Mirror writing is a type of writing that looks normal when viewed in a mirror. Ambulances often have the word **AMBULANCE** written in large mirrored text so that drivers in front of them can read it correctly in their rearview mirror. Interestingly, Leonardo da Vinci wrote most of his personal notes in mirror writing while using standard text for writing intended for others to read. Additionally, some children may use mirror writing when learning to write, although it is unclear why.

#456 If you're not a water sports person but want to try your hand at skiing or surfing, there is a whole world of adventure out there for you with sandboarding. There are many spots in the U.S. to go sandboarding, such as the Great Sand Dunes National Park in Colorado and many others. For the more serious sandboarder, there is a summer ski resort for sand skiing and sandboarding at Monte Kaolino in Bavaria, Germany. The yearly Sandboarding World Championship is held there.

More than Trivia   *Interesting Stories and Fascinating Facts*

Curiosities 135

#457 Although casket and coffin are often used interchangeably, they are two different things. Funeral homes generally only offer caskets, which are rectangular-shaped burial containers with rails on the side. Coffins, on the other hand, have six sides and are tapered slightly at the top to resemble the shape of a human body. In Western movies, you may have seen coffins outdoors leaning against a wall or rail before a gunfight.

#458 The 1883 eruption of the Krakatoa volcano in the Sudan Strait was heard as far away as 3,000 miles. The atmosphere's dust produced spectacular sunsets worldwide for many months. For several years following the eruption, it was reported that the moon appeared to be blue and sometimes green. This eruption also produced a Bishop's Ring (a diffuse brown or bluish halo) around the sun by day and a purple volcanic light at twilight.

#459 When the London Eye opened in 2000, it was the world's tallest Ferris wheel, also called an observation wheel, in the world at 443 feet tall. It has since been surpassed by the Star of Nanchang in China (525 feet), the Singapore Flyer (541 feet), and the High Roller in Las Vegas at 548 feet. However, because of the design of the London Eye, with the wheel only being supported on one side by an A-frame, it is still the tallest cantilevered design observation wheel.

#460 Japan has a unique beach called the *Hoshizuna no Hama* (Star Sand Beach), which contains tiny star-shaped exoskeletons of single-celled creatures called *Foraminifera* mixed in with the sand. These tiny creatures once lived in the sea and are one of the oldest fossils known to man. Local legend has it that the tiny stars were once the children of the Southern Cross and the North Star born in Okinawa's sea and were killed by a sea snake that left their skeletons behind.

Interesting Stories and Fascinating Facts **More** than **Trivia**

Curiosities

#461 The Great Molasses Flood occurred in January 1919, when a large storage tank with over 2 million gallons of molasses burst in Boston, Massachusetts. The wave of molasses rushed through the streets at about 35 miles per hour with a peak wave of 25 feet. The molasses flooded several blocks up to three feet deep in molasses. The molasses flood killed twenty-one people and injured 150. The area smelled of molasses for decades after that.

#462 The mysterious Georgia Guidestones near Elberton, Georgia, was a 19-foot high monument composed of five granite columns erected in 1980 engraved with 10 guidelines in 8 languages of how to restore society after an apocalypse. The monument was known as America's Stonehenge, and its origins were unknown. The local Chamber of Commerce said it was funded by an anonymous "small group of loyal Americans who believe in God" and lived outside Georgia. On July 6, 2022, one of the side stones was destroyed by an explosion. Out of safety concerns, the rest of the stones were destroyed by local officials.

#463 Forrest Fenn, an 80-year-old art dealer and author from Santa Fe, New Mexico, hid a treasure chest in 2010 worth up to $2 million to create a treasure hunt. Hidden in the Rocky Mountains, the chest contained gold nuggets, rare coins, and jewelry. Fenn provided three general clues and published a book called *The Thrill of the Chase* with a poem containing "10 or so" more clues. Over the years, hundreds of thousands searched for the treasure; unfortunately, five died during the pursuit. In June 2020, a 32-year-old medical student found the treasure, which weighed 22 pounds and measured 10 x 10 x 5 inches. However, the search for the treasure was not without controversy, conspiracy theories, and lawsuits. Fenn passed away in September 2020.

More than Trivia *Interesting Stories and Fascinating Facts*

Curiosities

#464 In 2016, while a 65-year-old woman in Wales was shopping, about 20,000 bees landed on her parked car because their queen was inside it. Beekeepers were sent out to remove the swarm, and they thought that was the end of it. She drove home and noticed that some bees had followed her the next day and were again on her car. The beekeepers were called out again to remove the bees though the queen was not found.

#465 The quietest place on earth is in Building 87 at Microsoft headquarters in Redmond, Washington. This specially designed room, an anechoic chamber, tests new equipment. The room is so quiet that you can hear your heartbeat, the sound of your blood flowing through your body, or even your joints grinding as you move. The noise level limit of human hearing is around 0 decibels, but the noise level in this chamber is -20.6 decibels. However, most people find being in a room like this quite unsettling. Orfield Labs in Minnesota has a similar room with a noise level of -9.4 decibels, but the longest anyone can stay inside it is only 45 minutes.

#466 In 1968, four bank employees of Nippon Trust Bank in Tokyo, Japan, were transporting 300 million yen (about $817,500) in a company car when they were robbed. The robber posed as a motorcycle cop that stopped them and told them he had received a warning that an explosive device had been planted in their car. The robber crawled under the car and came out moments later with smoke and flames coming from underneath the vehicle. The four bank employees exited the car when the robber entered and drove away. The smoke and flames were caused by a flare that the robber ignited under the vehicle. The robber later switched to another stolen car and transferred the money to it. The robber and the money were never found.

Interesting Stories and Fascinating Facts **More than Trivia**

Curiosities

#467   Some older or historic homes may have one of the stairway spindles (baluster) upside-down. One explanation for this says that the builders purposely installed one spindle upside-down to acknowledge that only God's creations are perfect. There is also an English superstition that claims an upside-down spindle prevents the devil from climbing the stairs and taking anyone on their deathbed.

#468   There are some pretty remote and interesting ATMs out there. The southernmost ATM is at the McMurdo Station, a U.S. science facility in the Antarctic that supports up to 1,200 people. Above the Arctic Circle, the northernmost ATM is in Barrow, Alaska (pop. 4,000). Interestingly, a gold-plated ATM/Vending Machine in Dubai dispenses 320 items made of gold, including gold bars and coins. Among the unique ATMs worldwide, there are also two whimsical ones. There is an ATM inside a large model of a pink Asian Elephant at the Dusit Zoo in Bangkok, Thailand. Lastly, you will find an ATM installed in a large pig structure at the Wiener Prater, a large public park in Vienna, Austria.

#469   In 1897, at the request of Indiana physician and amateur mathematician Edward J. Goodwin, the Indiana General Assembly tried to pass the Indiana Pi Bill based on Goodwin's unsupported math theories and his belief that he had solved a previously unsolvable math problem. The intent was to allow Indiana schools to teach his copyrighted (and convoluted) formula for free, and other states would have to pay royalties. Fortunately, the bill was shelved when Clarence A. Waldo, a visiting Purdue math professor, heard about the bill and spoke to the Senators about the error of Goodwin's theories. When asked if he would like to meet Goodwin, Waldo replied that he was already acquainted with as many crazy people as he cared to know.

More than Trivia   *Interesting Stories and Fascinating Facts*

Curiosities

#470 Despite the illusion that the Gateway Arch in St. Louis is taller than it is wide, it is precisely the same distance in both directions (630 feet).

#471 One million dollars in one-hundred-dollar bills weighs 22 pounds and will fit into a briefcase. A single bill of any U.S. currency weighs 1 gram, which is about 454 bills per pound.

#472 One in every eight people dream in black and white. The average person has 4-6 dreams every night but forgets 90% of them. In a lifetime, we spend about six years dreaming.

#473 Approximately one in every 200 men worldwide is a descendant of Genghis Khan, which amounts to around 16 million individuals. While there isn't any DNA available for Khan himself, other genetic evidence and research suggest a unique Y-chromosome lineage.

#474 The borders of Colorado are defined by 697 physical boundary markers connected by 697 straight border lines. Thus, it is not a 4-sided rectangle as it appears on a map, but its shape consisting of 697 sides is called a **hexahectaenneacontakaiheptagon**. The borders of Colorado were initially defined in 1861 by latitude and longitude. But when official surveys began in 1868 to establish the borders, they deviated in several places from the latitude and longitude. Later surveys tried to correct these errors, but in 1925, the Supreme Court ruled that the original surveyed borders would remain correct. The 697 boundary markers around the state's perimeter typically identify a change of direction in the border. The true shape of Colorado will remain a multi-sided polygon with a name consisting of 11 syllables and 30 letters.

Interesting Stories and Fascinating Facts   **More** than Trivia

Curiosities

#475 Many lipsticks contain a byproduct of fish scales called pearl essence or "pearlescence." It is what makes fish shimmery and lips (not fish lips) shiny. Most pearl essence comes from herring.

#476 In October 2022, a rare nickel sold for $4.2 million. This particular nickel was the Walton 1913 Liberty Head Nickel, and there are only 5 in existence. In 1919, Samuel Brown ran a magazine advertisement offering $500 for any of these nickels, and soon after that, he had all five nickels. The funny thing about Brown is that he was a U.S. Mint employee when he acquired all five nickels. Some speculate that he may have had them illegally printed and ran the ad to boost their value. The five nickels changed hands multiple times over the years, each gaining the nickname of the collector's last name that purchased it. So, check your change the next time you reach for a coin. You may have a small fortune in your pocket.

#477 There have been some uniquely named people throughout history. **Preserved Fish** was a shipping merchant born in 1766 in Massachusetts. His family name really was Fish, and Preserved is a Quaker name that refers to being preserved (saved) from sin. **Ima Hogg**, born in 1882, was known as "The First Lady of Texas." She was a philanthropist that owned works by Picasso and others. **John B. Goodenough**, born in Germany in 1922, was a physicist credited with identifying and developing the lithium-ion battery. **Guy Standing** is a British labor economist. **States Rights Gist** was a lawyer and a military general in the Civil War. His father, Nathaniel Gist, chose his son's name to reflect his own political viewpoint. Sometimes a person will change their name later in life. **Henry Lizardlover** of Hollywood, California, was born Henry Schifberg in 1954 but changed his name in 1986. He shares his home with his family of 30-50 iguanas.

More than **Trivia** *Interesting Stories and Fascinating Facts*

Curiosities

#478 One of the first uses of sunglasses was by Chinese judges in the 12th century to hide their facial expressions while questioning witnesses. These sunglasses were made from flat pieces of smoky quartz, which in Chinese is called *Ai Tai*, meaning dark clouds.

#479 Micronations are entities that claim sovereignty over physical territory but are not recognized by established governments. Individuals often start them due to disputes and declare secession from their legally recognized government. Micronations typically create their own flag and other aspects of a government. The nation they claim secession from generally tolerates or ignores them. One interesting example in the U.S. is the Conch Republic, located in southern Florida (ConchRepublic.com). They state that they "welcome all comers who understand the value of humor, community, and a passion for encouraging others to behave in a proud and foolish manner. The only requirement for entry is an understanding that to be in an alternate reality you have to participate in an alternate reality."

#480 It may look like a scene from a spooky movie, but in Centralia, Pennsylvania, smoke rising from the ground at a cemetery, and other locations, is a real phenomenon. A fire has been burning in the coal mines beneath the town since 1962, causing the population to dwindle from 1,000 in 1980 to just five people today. There are several theories about how the fire started, and state officials consider the area dangerous. In 1992, all real estate in the town was taken under eminent domain, and as the remaining residents pass away, their property will be claimed as well. However, the Ukranian Catholic church in the town is still in use and attended by people from nearby areas and some former residents. A geological survey has found that the church is built on solid rock and is not at risk of collapsing due to the underground fire.

Interesting Stories and Fascinating Facts   **More** than **Trivia**

Curiosities

#481   During the late 1990s, two researchers utilized mathematical modeling to identify 85 possible ways to tie a conventional tie.

#482   When we think about the desert, we think about large areas of sand like the Sahara Desert in Africa or the Mojave Desert in the western U.S. Technically, a desert indicates a barren area where little precipitation occurs. Because of that definition, there are also Polar deserts such as the Antarctic and the Arctic deserts.

#483   The World Association of Ugly People, which started in 1879, sponsors the annual Festival of the Ugly in Piobbico, Italy (pop. 1,837). The organization has 30,000 members worldwide, and its motto is "A person is what he is and not what he looks like." They fight against discrimination in the workplace based on looks, and they try to make society more aware of the problems of ugly people.

#484   Real estate developers contracted the Crescent Sign Company to build the large **HOLLYWOOD** sign in the Santa Monica Mountains overlooking Los Angeles in 1923. The sign initially read **HOLLYWOODLAND** and was intended to be a temporary advertisement for their real estate development. Originally made from wood, each letter was 30 feet wide and 50 feet high, with 4,000 light bulbs studded around it and a searchlight below it. The sign deteriorated over the years, and in 1949, the sign was repaired with wood and sheet metal, and the "LAND" part of the sign was removed. The structure again deteriorated and was replaced in 1978 with an all-steel design on a concrete foundation. The new letters were 44 feet tall and 31-39 feet wide. Nine donors gave $27,778 each for the work including Alice Cooper (in memory of Groucho Marx), Gene Autry, Hugh Hefner, Warner Bros. Records, and Andy Williams.

More than Trivia   *Interesting Stories and Fascinating Facts*

Curiosities

#485 50 billion tons of beach sand and fossil sand is used each year for construction. Desert sand, although plentiful, is not suitable for construction because of its composition.

#486 The Goodyear Blimp has two unique distinctions. In 1983, it was recognized as the "Official Bird of Redondo Beach, California," and, in 2019, was the first-ever non-human inductee into the College Football Hall of Fame.

#487 There is no reliable truth serum despite its portrayal in movies. Those who take such drugs can be more susceptible to suggestions and manipulation. During World War II, various drugs were tested as a potential truth serum, but the results were not significantly different from the effects of alcohol. Although subjects were more talkative, they weren't necessarily more honest.

#488 Do you ever wonder what happens to lost and unclaimed baggage from planes, trains, and buses? It likely winds up at the Unclaimed Baggage Center (UBC) retail store in Scottsboro, Alabama (pop. 15,578). More than a million people visit the 50,000-square-foot store yearly from every state and more than 40 countries. UBC is unlike a thrift store where people donate things to sell because they no longer want them. UBC sells items that people wanted but that got misplaced. Some of the more unique items they have seen have included a suite of armor, a 40-carat emerald ring, a bear pelt, an Egyptian burial mask, a four-foot-tall Hoggle goblin puppet, a Renaissance lute, Chinese opium scales, a Native American peace pipe, and a live rattlesnake. And, of course, many clothes and other items are available that people commonly take on vacations or business trips. *(https://www.unclaimedbaggage.com/)*

Curiosities

#489 In the U.S., the FDA classifies and regulates most deodorants as cosmetics but classifies antiperspirants as over-the-counter drugs.

Chapter 11

Companies

#490 A Polish company, Biotrem, makes edible tableware and cutlery out of wheat bran. They say it is suitable for serving hot and cold meals and can be used in traditional or microwave ovens. Biotrem makes about 15 million plates or bowls a year in various sizes. Their products are fully biodegradable through composting in 30 days. Or if you wanted to, you could eat them! They may not be very tasty by themselves, but with your condiment of choice or whipped cream, they would be more palatable.

#491 In 2012, two Italian brothers, Vincenzo and Giacomo Barbato, wanted to start their own clothing company. During their research, they discovered that Apple Computer had never trademarked Steve Jobs' well-known name. The company they established has a logo in the form of the letter "J" with a cutout and an apple-like leaf on top, similar to Apple's logo. Apple sued the brothers citing the similarity of their logo. The European Union's Intellectual Property Office sided with the Barbato brothers, saying that the letter "J" is not a food item, as Apple's logo, and cannot be a bite mark.

Companies

#492 William Wrigley Jr. started his business in Chicago in 1891 by selling scouring soap. He used incentives like baking powder to encourage people to buy his soap, but baking powder soon became more promising than soap. Wrigley continued his practice of giving free samples, this time of chewing gum, which became even more successful. As a result, he shifted his focus to chewing gum.

#493 The Volkswagen Plant in Wolfsburg, Germany, serves as their global headquarters and is one of the largest manufacturing plants in the world. Surprisingly, the best-selling product produced here is not cars but sausages - specifically, the Volkswagen currywurst. Volkswagen produces approximately 7 million sausages annually and makes its own ketchup to accompany the currywurst. While 40% of the currywurst is consumed at the restaurants located within its German factories, the rest is sold in supermarkets, football stadiums, and other external shops. This sausage is sold in 11 countries but is unavailable in the United States.

#494 In 1955, Quaker Oats Company launched a "Klondike Big Inch Land Promotion." The company placed a deed of land in each cereal box they distributed, offering the deed holders one square inch of land in the Canadian Yukon Territory. However, the deeds were not registered, making them legally invalid, and the deed holders never actually became property owners. This promotion inspired a Scrooge McDuck Comic Book story in 1956. In the story, Scrooge visits a square inch of land he owns in Texas and notices a prairie dog with engine oil on its feet, leading him to believe that oil is under his land. So, he sent Donald Duck and his kids to purchase cereal boxes from different parts of the country to acquire neighboring square inches of land and drill for oil on his property.

More than Trivia   *Interesting Stories and Fascinating Facts*

Companies

#495 Eternal Reefs is a company that incorporates a person's cremation ashes into a concrete, artificial reef ball to create a memorial to the deceased and a product that protects and preserves marine life. They use a patented mold system to mimic natural reef formations conducive to growing sea life. They have placed over 2,000 Eternal Reefs on the ocean floor in 25 locations off the Florida panhandle, the Gulf Coast, and the Atlantic Coast.

#496 Charles Entertainment Cheese III is the full name of the famous rodent mascot of the Chuck E. Cheese family restaurant chain. In 1977, Nolan Bushnell, the founder of Atari, attended an Amusement Park conference where he bought a costume that he believed to be a coyote for his planned restaurant, Coyote Pizza. When the costume arrived, he realized it was a rat costume with a long pink tail. Bushnell then changed the name of his planned restaurant to Rick Rat's Pizza. However, his business associates were not pleased with the name and changed it to Chuck E. Cheese. The rat mascot was later replaced with a child-friendly mouse mascot.

#497 When they started, the founders of Ben & Jerry's Ice Cream knew nothing about making ice cream or running a business. They took a $5 correspondence class from Penn State to learn how to make ice cream. To understand business, they read some brochures by the Small Business Administration they bought for 20 cents apiece. They initially considered selling bagels, but the restaurant equipment was too expensive. They had $12,000 to start their business - $4,000 each of them came up with and $4,000 they borrowed from the bank. They opened their first location in 1978 in a run-down gas station with a leaky room in Burlington, Vermont. By 1987 the company was worth $30 million, and in 2000 they sold the company to Unilever for $326 million.

Interesting Stories and Fascinating Facts   **More** than **Trivia**

Companies

#498 Loop Biotech, located in Delft, the Netherlands, offers a unique product called the "Living Cocoon" coffin they deliver across Europe. They use mycelium from nearby mushrooms and upcycled hemp fibers to grow the coffin in their factory within seven days. The coffin is then naturally dried, which makes it strong and stiff while only weighing 66 pounds. The Living Cocoon is approved for traditional burials and can be stored in a dry and ventilated space indefinitely. This eco-friendly product is biodegradable and, when buried in the ground, will "become one with nature" in 45 days.

#499 Despite its small physical size and population of just over 1 million, Delaware has over 1.6 million registered corporations. The large number of registered corporations, most without a physical location in the state, is due to their business-friendly laws and tax regulations. More than half of all publicly traded companies in the U.S. and over 65% of the Fortune 500 are incorporated in Delaware. Many well-known companies such as Amazon, Apple, Coca-Cola, Disney, General Motors, Google, Tesla, Verizon, and Walmart have taken advantage of Delaware's favorable business environment.

#500 Bill Hewlett and David Packard, both electrical engineers, started their business part-time in 1938 in a rented garage in Palo Alto, California. The location is now designated as a California Historical Landmark and marked with a plaque calling it the "Birthplace of Silicon Valley." They tossed a coin to determine if the company's name should be Hewlett-Packard or Packard-Hewlett. Packard won the toss, but he thought Hewlett-Packard sounded better. Their initial investment to start their business was $538. In 1939, their first full year in business, their total profit was $1,563 on revenues of $5,369. Their 2022 revenue was $63 billion.

More than Trivia *Interesting Stories and Fascinating Facts*

Companies

#501 A class action lawsuit against Walmart accused the retailer of misleading consumers by selling Fudge Mint cookies with neither fudge nor mint. A Chicago federal judge dismissed the case in 2023, stating that the product does not have to contain fudge or mint as long as it tastes like fudge and mint.

#502 In 2018, Domino's Pizza in Russia ran a promotion that gave customers 100 free pizzas a year for one hundred years if they got a Domino logo tattoo on a visible part of their body. Domino's planned to run the promotion for two months but hurriedly shut it down after five days because of the overwhelming response. After the pizza dust cleared, 350 customers had free pizza for life.

#503 The letters in the Swedish company IKEA stand for Ingvar Kamprad Elmtaryd Agunnaryd. Ingvar Kamprad is the company's founder; Elmtaryd is the farm where he grew up, and Agunnaryd is the nearby village. Always an entrepreneur, he started selling matches at age five and then expanded his business to include Christmas tree decorations, seeds, pens, and pencils. At 17, he founded IKEA as primarily a mail-order business.

#504 Blockbuster Video lives! As of late 2022, there is one remaining Blockbuster Video store in the U.S., and it's in Bend, Oregon. The store stocks about 1,200 titles and has about 4,000 members who regularly rent movies. The 2020 documentary, *The Last Blockbuster*, is about the store. They ran an online ad during the Super Bowl in February 2023, and as they make most of their money on merchandise, their sales went up 200%. You can view the ad on YouTube. It promises that this Blockbuster will still be there even after the world ends.

Interesting Stories and Fascinating Facts   **More** than **Trivia**

Companies

#505 A Swedish company called Corvid Cleaning has a program to train wild crows to pick up litter, specifically cigarette butts, in exchange for a food treat. The birds are to place the litter in a special bin where they will, in turn, get their treat. They have used Hooded Crows but plan to work with Magpies and Jackdaws.

#506 In March 2022, McDonald's temporarily closed its 850 locations in Russia due to Russia's invasion of Ukraine. Despite this, they continued to pay all 60,000 employees during the closure. However, in May 2022, the company announced that the closures would be permanent, and they were planning to sell all of their stores in the country. Meanwhile, they will continue to pay their employees until the sale is finalized.

#507 Costa Coffee is a British coffeehouse chain with over 3,400 stores in 31 countries. They are the largest coffeehouse chain in the UK and the second largest worldwide, behind Starbucks, which has over 33,000 stores in 80 countries. Interestingly, Costa Coffee employs a coffee taster named Gennaro Pelliccia, who had his tongue insured for 10 million pounds ($12 million+ USD) with Lloyds of London in 2009.

#508 Domino's Pizza started in 1960 when two brothers, Tom and James Monaghan, bought an existing pizza restaurant chain called DomiNick's, in Ypsilanti, Michigan, from Dominick DeVarti. The business demanded a lot of time, and within eight months, James had to decide whether to leave his job as a full-time postman or devote all of his time to their new business. He kept his post office job and traded half of the business to Tom for the Volkswagen Beetle they used for pizza deliveries. Tom retired in 1998, sold 93 percent of the company to Bain Capital for about $1 billion, and was no longer involved in the company's day-to-day operations.

More than Trivia   *Interesting Stories and Fascinating Facts*

Companies

#509 Jeff Bezos started his online business from his garage in Bellevue, Washington, in 1994 as an online bookseller. Now known as Amazon.com, his original idea for his business name was Cadabra.com (like Abracadabra). He decided to change it because Cadabra sounded too much like cadaver. He liked the idea of naming his company after the Amazon River because it is by far the largest river in the world, and he planned on making his online business the largest bookstore in the world.

#510 Yahoo!, a web services company, was founded in January 1994 by Electrical Engineering students Jerry Yang and David Filo at Stanford University. It was initially named "Jerry and David's Guide to the World Wide Web" as a directory of other websites. They renamed their site Yahoo! in April 1994 and, by the end of the year, had over one million hits. There is an exclamation mark (!) at the end of the word Yahoo for trademark reasons. Yahoo had been previously trademarked by a company that made barbecue sauce, so the Yahoo! founders added a '!' to end of the company name.

Interesting Stories and Fascinating Facts   *More* than *Trivia*

Chapter 12

Fun & Games

#511 The European-style Roulette table layout has a single zero, whereas the American style has a double zero. But in either case, if you add up all the numbers (0-36) on the Roulette wheel, it adds up to 666.

#512 The Pinata is of Chinese origin. It was shaped like a cow or ox. It was decorated with symbols and colors meant to produce a favorable climate for the coming growing season. It was filled with five types of seeds and then hit with sticks of various colors.

#513 The Lego company began in the workshop of Danish carpenter Ole Kirk Christiansen. He started making wooden toys in 1932, and in 1934, his company was called Lego, which is from the Danish phrase *leg godt*, which means "play well." In 1947, Lego started making plastic toys and, in 1949, began making an early version of interlocking bricks called Automatic Binding Bricks. Lego pieces from all varieties and years still interlock with those today. In 2021, Lego was the world's largest toy company, producing over 600 billion Lego parts.

Interesting Stories and Fascinating Facts   **More** than Trivia

Fun & Games

#514 Though jigsaw puzzles were initially made from wood, a jigsaw was never used to cut them.

#515 The Kingda Ka was the world's tallest roller coaster in 2005 when it opened at Six Flags Great Adventure in New Jersey. It reaches a height of 456 feet before dropping 418 feet, reaching its top speed of 128 mph in 3.5 seconds. The world's fastest roller coaster is the Formula Rossa in the United Arab Emirates which reaches a top speed of 149 mph in 4.9 seconds.

#516 To win at Monopoly, remember the goal is not to get the most money but to bankrupt your opponent. One top player recommends getting the orange properties (St. James Place, Tennessee Avenue, and New York Avenue) and loading them up with hotels. The logic is that these properties are just down the board from Jail, and if your rival rolls the popular 6 or 8 from Jail, they will end up on the orange properties.

#517 Ruth Handler, the wife of Mattel's co-founder Elliot Handler, once mentioned to her husband that there may be a market for an adult-bodied doll for children to play with. Elliot and the Mattel directors were not interested. At that time, most dolls were infant dolls. But on a trip to Europe in 1956 with her children Barbara and Kenneth, she came across an adult-figured doll she had in mind called Bild Lilli. The Lilli doll was based on a blonde bombshell character in a comic strip for the newspaper *Bild*. She bought three dolls and redesigned them after returning to the U.S. and sold Mattel on the idea. Barbie (named after Handler's daughter) was introduced at the American International Toy Fair on March 9, 1959, the doll's official birthday. Barbie's full name is Barbara Millicent Roberts. They sold about 350,000 in the first year, and in 2020, Mattel sold $1.35 billion of Barbie dolls and accessories.

More than Trivia *Interesting Stories and Fascinating Facts*

Fun & Games

#518 The World Kite Museum in Long Beach, Washington, has over 1,500 kites from 26 countries worldwide.

#519 The first permanent amusement park was founded in 1895 as Sea Lion Park at Coney Island in New York. It was one of the first to charge admission to the park and sell tickets for rides within the park.

#520 Goerge Lerner, the inventor of Mr. Potato Head, used potatoes from his mother's garden to create dolls for his younger sisters. He used grapes for eyes and carrots for noses to create his funny face man. From this came Mr. Potato Head with pushpin plastic parts to be stuck into a real potato. Lerner sold the idea to Hassenfeld Brothers (later called Hasbro), and Mr. Potato Head went into production on May 1, 1952, and sold originally for $.0.98. Mr. Potato Head was the first toy advertised on television and the first ad aimed at children. Hasbro sold over one million kits in the first year. They began including a plastic potato body with the toy kit in 1964.

#521 Hello Kitty is a fictional character created by designer Yuko Shimizu in 1974 and is currently owned by the Japanese company Sanrio. The character first appeared on a vinyl coin purse in 1975 and in the U.S. in 1976. With over 50,000 Hello Kitty branded products, the franchise generates over $8 billion in revenue annually. Hello Kitty is described as a kind-hearted girl named Kitty White, born in London's suburbs. Kitty's distinctive features are her red bow and lack of a visible mouth, which Sanrio has explained in two ways. Firstly, they want people to feel and react to Hello Kitty, projecting their emotions onto her. Secondly, they say that Kitty "speaks from the heart." Although, the current designer claims that Kitty has a mouth hidden by her fur.

Interesting Stories and Fascinating Facts **More** than **Trivia**

Fun & Games

#522 Today over 20,000 varieties of glitter are manufactured in many different colors, sizes, and materials.

#523 The Hokey Pokey dance (Hokey Cokey in the UK) originated in a British folk dance with variants dating back to 1826.

#524 In the game Scrabble, if a player uses all seven of their tiles at one time, it is called a "bingo." In addition to getting the score of all your tiles, you also get a premium of 50 points.

#525 The board game Monopoly is based on The Landlord's Game, created by Lizzie Magie in 1903. Charles Darrow discovered the game and began distributing it as Monopoly. Maggie sold her patent rights for the game to Parker Brothers for $500, and Parker Brothers began marketing the game in 1935. The game has now sold over 275 million copies.

More than Trivia   *Interesting Stories and Fascinating Facts*

Chapter 13

Culture, Customs, & Laws

#526 Dutch police cars carry a teddy bear to help comfort a child who has seen or experienced a crime or accident. It's remarkable how much a therapeutic teddy bear can help.

#527 Patchouli is a vital component of East Asian incense. The popularity of patchouli oil and incense surged in the 1960s and 1970s, primarily because of the hippie movement. Interestingly, Indonesia produces over 90% of the world's patchouli oil.

#528 Men must wear tight-fitting swimsuits at most swimming pools in France. Check with the local rules before you go, or keep a tight one packed just in case. The main reason is that people often wear long, loose-fitting swim trunks as shorts during daily activities. Those trunks are likelier to pick up dirt and bacteria than tight swim trunks and pollute the water. Tight swimsuits may also pick up dirt and bacteria, but they are less likely to be worn as casual clothes during the day.

Culture, Customs, & Laws

#529 Hawaii has a law prohibiting anyone from "introducing, keeping or breeding" mongooses unless they have a Hawaii Department of Agriculture permit. Fines run from $250 to $1,000 for each mongoose. Mongooses were initially introduced into Hawaii by sugar cane farmers so that they would kill the rats in their fields. But the mongooses prefer the native bird and turtle population rather than the rats, so they have become a big problem in Hawaii.

#530 There always seems to be a loophole for almost any law that the government passes. One example is "tariff engineering," which involves designing products overseas to allow them to be imported with lower tariffs. For example, Columbia Sportswear adds small pockets (Nurse's pockets) below the waistline on their shirts to reduce import costs. Ford tried to modify their Transit Vans made in Spain to reduce the tariff from 25% to 2.5%, which would then be unmodified once the vans were in the United States. But it didn't work, and they faced penalties and interest. Converse adds a layer of felt to the bottom of their sneakers to classify them as slippers and reduce tariffs from 37.5% to 3%.

#531 Most chewing gum sales have been banned in Singapore since 1992 because of vandalism caused by discarded chewing gum. It was put in keyholes and elevator lift buttons in public housing, on the door sensors of the public railway system trains, and littered throughout the country, causing increased cleaning and maintenance costs. Since then, the ban has been partially lifted, with gum being chewed for dental health being allowed. But even then, it could only be sold by a dentist or pharmacist who had to keep a record of the buyer's names. Lee Kuan Yew, Prime Minister of Singapore, once responded to a concern that laws like the chewing gum ban would stifle people's creativity. He replied, "If you can't think because you can't chew, try a banana."

More than Trivia   *Interesting Stories and Fascinating Facts*

Culture, Customs, & Laws

#532 The coffee break originated in the late 19th century in Stoughton, Wisconsin, with the wives of Norwegian immigrants. The city celebrates this every year with the Stoughton Coffee Break Festival.

#533 In ancient royal courts, a cup-bearer was a highly respected and reliable individual who served drinks at the king's table. This was a prestigious and lucrative position but it also carried significant risks. Cup-bearers were responsible for protecting the king from poison, sometimes requiring them to taste the drinks before serving them.

#534 A new law in Béziers, France, requires dog owners to have their pet's DNA on file and a "genetic" passport issued. Mayor Robert Ménard is tired of seeing the poop in his town left behind by the dog's owners. The law allows for any poop found on the streets to be gathered and analyzed for DNA, with the results sent to law enforcement to match with a pet registry. Law-breaking pet owners will be located and charged for the cleanup.

#535 First-footing is a custom in Scotland and northern England that occurs on the first day of the year. The "first-foot" is the first person to enter the home of a household on New Year's Day and is seen as a bringer of good fortune for the coming year. Generally, a tall, dark-haired male is preferred over a man with light hair or even a woman. Women and light or red-haired men are considered very unlucky for this occasion. The first-foot should bring a selection of gifts for the household, including a silver coin; shortbread or a black bun (a type of fruit cake); salt; coal; and a drink, usually whisky. They represent prosperity, food, flavor, warmth for the house, and good cheer – the whisky is used to toast the new year.

Interesting Stories and Fascinating Facts   **More** than Trivia

Culture, Customs, & Laws

#536 It is against the law to throw rocks at a train in Wisconsin. Section 943.07 paragraph 3 of Wisconsin state law says, "Whoever intentionally throws, shoots or propels any stone, brick or other missile at any railroad train, car, caboose or engine is guilty of a Class B misdemeanor."

#537 Many communities have laws protecting animals; the Swiss even extend this protection to an animal's social needs. It is illegal in Switzerland to keep certain social animals, such as guinea pigs and gerbils, on their own. This means that because guinea pigs and gerbils are social animals and they could get lonely, you cannot own only one – you must own two or more.

#538 The "Democracy Sausage" is a sausage served on a slice of bread at a polling place food stand in Australia on election day. Voting is mandatory in Australia, and elections are held on Saturdays, resulting in high voter turnout. Most polling places are at schools, churches, or community centers and many of them set up food stands to sell various food items to benefit their organization.

#539 Waulking songs are a type of Scottish folk song sung in Gaelic by a group of women while they worked on cleansing cloth, a process called "waulking." This process was used from the 1400s until the mid-20th century. It produced a smooth, tight, water-repellent fabric, such as duffel cloth. While singing the songs, one person sang the verse while the other sang the chorus, often made up of vocables like "na na na na" or "hey hey hey." You may have seen this practice on TV shows like in Season 1 of *Outlander* and the Season 9 Christmas Special of *Call the Midwife*. Waulking was also called fulling, tucking, and walking. Surnames such as Fuller, Tucker, and Walker, became popular for people that did this work.

More than Trivia   *Interesting Stories and Fascinating Facts*

Culture, Customs, & Laws

#540 In 2021, after 30 years of forced sterilization to control their population growth, Chinese birthrates have fallen drastically. Now China wants more children, and hospitals typically refuse vasectomies because of the country's new family-planning rules.

#541 In the United Kingdom, the Licensing Act of 1872 makes it illegal to be intoxicated while in control of a horse, cow, steam engine, or carriage. It is also prohibited to carry a loaded firearm while under the influence. Breaking this law can result in a fine of up to $250 or imprisonment for up to 51 weeks.

#542 In many parts of the world, using your left hand for some things is considered bad manners. For instance, you shouldn't eat with it, shake someone's hand, or give someone something with it. This is because, in many countries, the left hand is used in the bathroom to wipe. So, as always, know your customs before you travel.

#543 Bart FM Droog came up with the idea of the "Lonely Funeral Project" after he was appointed city poet for Groningen, The Netherlands, in 2001. People died anonymously in his city each year, unclaimed by friends or family. He began to attend these lonely funerals, reading a poem inspired by whatever details could be found about the deceased. Coincidentally, civil servant Ger Frits of Amsterdam had started honoring the lonely dead in Amsterdam at about the same time. He would arrange a simple funeral with flowers, music, and pallbearers. Poet Frank Starik of Amsterdam heard about the Lonely Funeral Project and arranged with Frits to incorporate an original poem at the funerals of the lonely deceased in Amsterdam. This concept has spread to other cities, and there is now a competition for the best lonely funeral poem written each year.

Interesting Stories and Fascinating Facts **More than Trivia**

Culture, Customs, & Laws

#544 Bear wrestling is not allowed in Alabama, nor can you buy or sell a bear for bear wrestling. This falls under the "Offenses against public health and morals. Section 13A-12-5 - Unlawful bear exploitation," a Class B felony.

#545 It is against the law to curse a player or official at a sporting event in Massachusetts if you are 16 or older. Part IV, Title I, Chapter 272, Section 36A of Massachusetts law says, "Whoever, having arrived at the age of sixteen years, directs any profane, obscene or impure language or slanderous statement at a participant or an official in a sporting event, shall be punished by a fine of not more than fifty dollars."

#546 If you have ever been in a home built in the late 1920s through the 1970s that has yet to be updated, you have probably seen the blue, green, pink, or yellow bathroom tile, toilets, and sinks. But did you know that toilet paper was available in various bright colors starting in the late 1960s? It became more scarce in the 1980s due to concern about the dyes used on toilet paper and because decorating tastes changed as well. But it is available online if you still want those retro colors for your decor or as a novelty gift.

#547 The government gives Expectant mothers in Finland a "Maternity Box" with about 60 products for the newborn baby. It includes clothes, diapers, personal care products, a picture book, a cuddly toy, and more. It even comes with a foam mattress that fits inside the box, becoming a simple crib for the baby to sleep in. Baby bottles are not included in the box to encourage breastfeeding. The Maternity Box began in 1938 for low-income families but was expanded in 1949 to include all families. Mothers can opt to take a cash grant instead of the box, but the value of the Maternity Box is much more than the cash.

More than Trivia   *Interesting Stories and Fascinating Facts*

Culture, Customs, & Laws

#548 Have you ever avoided answering the door when an unwelcome or unfamiliar visitor shows up? The practice is known as *Irusu* in Japanese culture.

#549 A coin left on the grave of a military veteran is a sign of respect for the deceased and, depending on the coin denomination has a special meaning. A penny indicates that the person visited the grave. A nickel indicates that the person attended boot camp with the deceased. A dime indicates that the person served with the deceased in the military. A quarter indicates that the person was present when the veteran died.

#550 Americans, on average, watch about 2 hours and 45 minutes of TV daily. Older or unemployed people watch more, and parents of young children watch less. Residents in Alaska, Idaho, Maine, Montana, New Mexico, Utah, Vermont, and Washington watch less than average. Residents of Alabama, Arkansas, Delaware, Georgia, Kentucky, Louisiana, Mississippi, North Carolina, North Dakota, Nevada, Oklahoma, Pennsylvania, Rhode Island, South Carolina, and West Virginia watch more.

#551 The word *ninja* comes from Japan and means "invisible one." Ninjas were skilled in guerrilla warfare, espionage, and surveillance. They were experts in infiltration and wore disguises to complete their tasks. Unlike the samurai, who followed a code of honor and inherited their nobility, ninjas were mainly from the lower classes and used dishonorable tactics. However, samurai sometimes hired ninjas for tasks that went against the samurai's moral code. Although many believe that ninjas always wore black clothing, this is untrue. They were masters of disguise and could blend in with civilian clothes or any attire that helped them accomplish their mission.

Interesting Stories and Fascinating Facts **More than Trivia**

Culture, Customs, & Laws

#552 Americans are the highest users of paper towels in the home compared to people in other countries. People in the Middle East prefer reusable cloth towels, and people in Europe prefer reusable cleaning sponges.

#553 There is no official language at the federal level for the United States. However, some individual states list English as their official language. Although English is the most commonly used language, more than 300 languages are spoken in the United States.

#554 There is an unwritten rule among British clowns that you don't copy the look of another clown. To ensure this compliance, Clowns International has an Egg Registry where a clown's face is painted on a ceramic egg, showing their unique identity. Initially, the clown face was painted on real, emptied-out chicken eggs when this practice started in 1946.

#555 In Venice, Italy, feeding pigeons has been prohibited since 2008. Those who disobey the law can be fined up to $900, required to do community service, or even sent to jail. Pigeons are viewed as a problem in the city because they can cause damage to buildings, contaminate food, and increase maintenance costs due to their droppings.

#556 Since 1678, the town of Wycombe (pop. 75,814), in southern England has practiced a tradition known as "Weighing the Mayor." The ceremony is in full public view and on the same scale since the 1800s. This ceremony aims to determine whether the mayor has gained weight, implying that they have done so at the taxpayers' expense. The actual weight is not disclosed, but the town crier announces, "And no more!" or "And some more!" to indicate the results.

More than **Trivia**   *Interesting Stories and Fascinating Facts*

Culture, Customs, & Laws

#557 The modern-day flip-flop became popular in the U.S. as soldiers returning from World War II brought the Japanese version, called *zori*, with them.

#558 Non-Profit bingo games in North Carolina cannot last more than five hours at a time. The law states "Licensed non-profit agencies are allowed to operate no more than twice a week with games being 48 hours apart and no longer than five hours per session."

#559 Utah had the country's largest median home size of 2,800 sq. ft. in 2022. The next four were Colorado (2,464), Idaho (2,311), Wyoming (2,285), and Delaware (2,277). Twenty-seven states have a median home size of at least 2,000 sq. ft. The five smallest median home sizes are Hawaii (1,164), New York (1,490), Iowa (1,623), Maine (1,680), and Illinois (1,700).

#560 Self-service gas pumps have been popular since the 1970s, but New Jersey is the only state that does not offer them. In fact, the Garden State has outlawed self-service gas pumps since 1949. Oregon has had a similar law since 1951 until they passed a new law in 2023 that says half of the gas pumps must be self-service, and gas stations cannot charge more for full service.

#561 In 2008, Mayor Gerard Lalanne of Sarpourenx, France, issued a decree saying no one could die within the city limits unless you had previously purchased a burial plot in the city. He threatened severe punishment for transgressors. This was primarily a symbolic protest because even though the small village cemetery was becoming overcrowded, a local judge rejected the city's request to use farmland for burial.

Interesting Stories and Fascinating Facts **More than Trivia**

Culture, Customs, & Laws

#562   It is against the law in South Carolina to operate a dance hall within one-fourth mile of a cemetery. Section 52-13-20 of South Carolina Code of Laws.

#563   The national animal of Scotland is the unicorn, a mythical creature. Many countries have a national animal that symbolizes or embodies some of that country's best qualities. The unicorn represents strength, courage, nobility, and purity - attributes the Scottish people embrace and hold dear.

#564   A French court intervened in 2015 to prevent new parents from naming their baby girl Nutella after the popular hazelnut spread. The judge said the name was not in the child's best interests and that a name such as Nutella "can only lead to teasing or disparaging thoughts." The judge ordered the baby to be named Ella instead. There are only a few naming restrictions in the United States, which are left to each state. Most states limit the number of characters in a name, and some ban obscenities as a name. Some states, such as Kentucky and others, have no restrictions for picking a name.

#565   The Navajo people have a wonderful tradition called a "First Laugh Ceremony" (A'wee Chi'deedloh). They believe that when a baby is first born, they live in a spirit world with the Holy People. The child's first laugh is a sacred event that indicates they have made the transition to the physical world to live with their earthly family. The person who inspired the baby's first laugh has an honored role as the organizer of the First Laugh Ceremony. The baby is considered the ceremony host and, with their parent's help, gives gifts to those in attendance, particularly rock salt. Salt used to be rare, and this gift signifies a great act of generosity, an important virtue to the Navajo people.

More than Trivia   *Interesting Stories and Fascinating Facts*

Culture, Customs, & Laws

#566 "Where's the Beef?" is a phrase from Wendy's 1984 ad that mocked a competitor's large bun - small patty burger. 82-year-old (at the time) actress Clara Peller, who said the line, was supposed to say, "Where is all the beef?" but struggled due to her emphysema. It has since become a catchphrase for questioning the substance of an idea or product. Walter Mondale successfully used it in a televised presidential debate against Gary Hart in 1984.

Interesting Stories and Fascinating Facts   **More** than Trivia

Culture, Customs, & Laws

More than Trivia *Interesting Stories and Fascinating Facts*

Chapter 14

History & Language

#567 In the 18th century, King George I of England ruled that all pigeon poop belonged to the Crown because the droppings contained saltpeter, an essential ingredient in making gunpowder. He even posted guards at strategic pigeon perching locations to protect the poo.

#568 The origin of the phrase "sweats like a pig" is uncertain. Pigs have very few sweat glands and cool off by rolling in mud. One explanation for the phrase is the shape molten iron takes when poured on sand, which resembles a sow and her piglets, hence the term "pig iron." As the iron cools, moisture beads form on it, indicating it is safe to handle.

#569 During World War II, the Japanese gained control of the rubber plantations in the Dutch East Indies, which was the source of 90% of America's raw rubber. As a result, the U.S. government added rubber to the list of rationed items, and citizens were encouraged to donate unused scrap rubber for recycling. Scrap rubber included old tires, garden hoses, rubber raincoats, and shoes.

History & Language

#570 In preparation for air attacks on major cities during World War II, the British government printed over 2 million motivational posters called "Keep Calm and Carry On." However, these posters were hardly ever displayed, and the majority were recycled in the "Paper Salvage" campaign to help the war effort. You may have come across other items that use the phrase "Keep Calm and" like "Keep Calm and Call Mom" or "Keep Calm and Wash Your Hands."

#571 State historian of South Dakota Doane Robinson came up with the idea for a National Memorial at Mount Rushmore in 1923. His initial idea was to use American West heroes instead of presidents, but sculptor Gutzon Borglum felt it should have a broader appeal with more recognizable figures. So instead of Lewis and Clark, Buffalo Bill Cody, and others, presidents Washington, Jefferson, Roosevelt, and Lincoln were chosen. Each president was originally going to be shown from head to waist, but lack of funding cut the project short.

#572 Nazi Germany launched "Operation Bernhard" during World War II, creating counterfeit British paper money to finance their operations. By the war's end, they had produced over $150 million of counterfeit British pounds, with over $20 million in circulation. Due to the prevalence of counterfeit notes, the Bank of England ceased releasing 10-pound notes and above in 1943. In 1957, they introduced a new 5-pound note, followed by the 10-pound note in 1964, with higher denominations to follow. In 1958, several boxes of counterfeit money were discovered at the bottom of Lake Toplitz in Austria, with one bank official describing it as "the most dangerous ever seen" due to its quality. The Nazis also attempted to forge U.S. dollars, and though the printing and engraving were excellent, the paper used was inferior to the genuine note.

More than Trivia   *Interesting Stories and Fascinating Facts*

History & Language

#573 To protest the Nazi occupation of Norway, Norwegians wore paperclips on cuffs and lapels. One paperclip design was of Norwegian origin, so this simple act, the "Paperclip Protest," symbolized Norwegian unity against the Nazi occupation of their country.

#574 Before Queen Elizabeth II married Philip Mountbatten in 1947, the government granted her 200 extra ration coupons to buy her wedding dress. Hundreds of brides-to-be across the country also donated their ration coupons to the Queen at this time. However, as it was illegal to give away your coupons, she returned each of them along with a thank you note.

#575 In 1946, Soviet schoolchildren gifted William Harriman, the American ambassador to the Soviet Union, a hand-carved wooden replica of the Great Seal of the United States. This replica hung in the ambassador's official residence in Moscow for seven years until it was discovered to contain an advanced listening device named "The Thing." It was surprising that the device had no power source or visible wires. The Thing was created by Soviet inventor Leon Theremin, famous for inventing the musical instrument known as the Theremin.

#576 At the siege of Weinsberg, Germany, in 1140 AD, a surrender was negotiated before the final assault of King Conrad III. As part of the agreement, the wives and other women there were allowed to leave with whatever they could carry on their shoulders. Rather than household goods, the women of the city came out carrying the men on their shoulders. The king granted them favor and did not go back on his promise. This story of loyalty and cunning on the part of the wives to save their husbands became known as the "Loyal Wives of Weinsberg."

Interesting Stories and Fascinating Facts **More** than **Trivia**

History & Language

#577 When the National Prohibition Act, also called the Volstead Act, was enacted in 1919, Walgreens Drug store had just 20 stores. By 1930, it had 397 stores, partly due to selling prescribed alcohol, mainly whiskey, allowed under the Prohibition Act.

#578 Liechtenstein's national flag features two horizontal bands of equal size; the top band is dark blue, while the bottom band is red. During the 1936 Summer Olympics, they discovered that the country's flag was identical to Haiti's. As a result, in 1937, they redesigned their flag by adding the prince's crown near the left edge of the upper blue band.

#579 Though the Constitution requires a president to take a salary, four presidents have refused it in whole or part. John F. Kennedy donated his presidential and congressional (14 years) salary to charity. Herbert Hoover gave his salary to various charities and some to his staff. George Washington refused to take his salary, and Donald Trump donated his to various federal departments.

#580 There is a hidden chamber called the Hall of Records behind the four carved faces on Mount Rushmore. Sculptor Gutzon Borglum had lofty plans for this chamber, including a bronze eagle with a 38-foot wing span above the entrance. The project was halted after a year, with only a 70-foot cavern blasted into the mountain. The project sat unfinished for almost 60 years when a scaled-back version of the original plan was initiated. Today, the chamber contains 16 panels about Mount Rushmore and why each president was chosen. It also includes the text of the Bill of Rights, the U.S. Constitution, and the Declaration of Independence. Not available to the public, it is a historical record for future generations.

More than **Trivia**   *Interesting Stories and Fascinating Facts*

History & Language

#581 *Tsundoku* is a word in Japanese that describes collecting too many books and not reading them. The term combines parts of *tsunde-oku*, meaning to stack and leave things for later, and *dokusho*, which means reading books.

#582 Onomatopoeia (on-uh-mat-uh-pee-uh) is using a word that phonetically resembles or suggests the sound it describes. Some examples are chirp, hiccup, honk, meow, moo, oink, and ribbit. Comic strips often use onomatopoeia by throwing in an occasional bam, pow, or ker-splash.

#583 The longest word in English is 189,819 letters long and takes about 3 hours to attempt to pronounce. It is a word that is not in any dictionary and describes the chemical composition of titin, the largest known protein. The longest published word is 1,909 letters long and describes the chemical name of *E. coli* TrpA (P0A877). The fifth longest word is *supercalifragilisticexpialidocious*, the nonsense word we all learned as a kid in school and was made famous in the movie *Mary Poppins*.

#584 Another mystery surrounding the assassination of President John F. Kennedy (JFK) is that his brain went missing after his death. During the autopsy, his brain was placed in a jar and moved to a stainless-steel container. This container was transferred to the National Archives in a secure room. By 1966, JFK's brain was missing from the National Archives. Some say the brain was stolen to cover up that there was a second shooter besides Oswald. Others say that JFK's brother was responsible for the brain theft to cover up the president's medical condition. Though thousands of records of the assassination were released on December 15, 2022, they did not provide any new answers for some of the mysteries of that fateful day in November 1963.

Interesting Stories and Fascinating Facts   **More** than **Trivia**

History & Language

#585 On April 18, 1930, listeners tuned into the popular BBC News radio show at 8:45 PM, expecting to hear the regular evening news bulletin. Instead, they heard the announcement: "Good evening. Today is Good Friday. There is no news." Then, the station played piano music for the rest of the 15-minute show.

#586 The letter "A" is the second most popular letter in our alphabet (second only to "E"). But curiously enough, the letter "A" does not appear in any of the first 999 numbers spelled out – one, two, three, four, twenty-seven, one hundred ninety-two, etc. It first appears when you get to 1,000 (one thousand). Even the uncommon letter "X" appears more than two hundred times (six, sixteen, sixty, etc.).

#587 President William Henry Harrison had the shortest presidency in history, dying of pneumonia just 31 days after his inauguration as the 9th president of the United States. He was the paternal grandfather of the 23rd president, Benjamin Harrison. In 1811, at 38, he led a military force in the Battle near the Tippecanoe River in Indiana. He earned the nickname "Old Tippecanoe." Harrison's running mate in the 1840 election was John Tyler, and their campaign slogan was "Tippecanoe and Tyler Too."

#588 Christopher Columbus may have landed in Cuba, Jamaica, and other Caribbean islands, thinking he was in Asia, but he never set foot on North American soil. When the Europeans finally did "discover" North America, large groups of people were already living on the continent, presumably migrating from Russia to Alaska across the Bering Land Bridge over 15,000 years ago, which was passable then. Over time, these people traveled south and across all areas of the modern-day United States.

More than Trivia   *Interesting Stories and Fascinating Facts*

History & Language

#589 A knocker-upper was a profession mainly active from the 1800s and lasting into the early 20th century, primarily in Britain and Ireland. As alarm clocks were expensive and unreliable during this time, the job of the knocker-upper was to walk around town waking people up so they could get to work on time. They would use a short, heavy stick to knock on clients' doors or long, light sticks to reach windows on upper floors. Some even used a pea-shooter to reach upper windows. Each knocker-upper served up to one hundred clients.

#590 Fearing German bombing attacks on Paris in World War I, the French devised an innovative way to prevent the destruction of Paris and, inevitably, the fall of France. They decided to build a fake Paris 15 miles north of the real Paris. They began the work in 1917 to construct several life-size replicas of Parisian landmarks along with working street lights and a railway. They felt this plan may have worked because World War I aircraft technology was crude, and bombing was often done at night. The conflict ended before the fake city was complete, so it's hard to say whether the plan would have worked. But what a great idea.

#591 The Rosetta Stone is a fragment of a larger stone containing a decree from King Ptolemy V Epiphanes of Egypt. The decree is written in three different types of language called scripts. The scripts are two types of Ancient Egyptian, and one is Ancient Greek. The Rosetta Stone is important because deciphering it is the key to understanding hieroglyphic writing. The Rosetta Stone is 3 ft 8 in high, 2 ft 5.8 in wide, and 11 in thick and weighs almost 1,700 lb. The stone has been on display in the British Museum since 1802 and is the museum's most visited single object. Other stone decrees, called Ptolemaic decrees, were discovered in the same period, which aided in understanding hieroglyphic writing.

Interesting Stories and Fascinating Facts **More** than **Trivia**

History & Language

#592 Originally built in 1921, the Tomb of the Unknown Soldier in Arlington National Cemetery contains the body of an unknown American soldier from World War I who typifies the soul of America and the supreme sacrifice of her heroic dead. Unknown soldiers from other wars were added later. Today it is a sarcophagus decorated with three wreaths on each side panel (north and south). On the front (east), three figures represent Peace, Victory, and Valor. The back (west) features the inscription: "Here rests in honored glory an American soldier known but to God."

#593 During World War II, allied forces dropped thousands of bombs on Germany, many of which never exploded and are discovered yearly across Germany. Weighing in at 4,000 pounds, the blockbuster bomb by Britain's Royal Air Force was one of the largest bombs used in World War II. In August 2017, near Frankfurt's Goethe University, the discovery of one of these unexploded blockbuster bombs led to the evacuation of 65,000 people while the bomb could be diffused. Then on Christmas Day, 2015, fifty-four thousand people were evacuated in Augsburg while one of these blockbuster bombs was diffused.

#594 Though recycling and repurposing existing products is trendy nowadays, it was popular in the 1930s and 1940s for frugality and necessity. Material for clothing was scarce then, and women started using the cloth bags their husbands brought home filled with seeds, feed, and flour, to make clothes, towels, curtains, and such. The early bags were very plain, with little or no design. As the bags became more in demand, manufacturers started marketing to the wife with bright colors and printed designs. Soon, there were national sewing contests for women to show off their skills and for manufacturers to show off their designs.

More than Trivia   *Interesting Stories and Fascinating Facts*

History & Language

#595 The name America is derived from Amerigo Vespucci, an Italian merchant, explorer, and navigator. Between 1497 and 1504, he participated in at least two voyages that took him to South America, which he deemed "A New World."

#596 Before there were jay-walkers, there were jay-drivers. "Jay" in this context refers to a greenhorn or novice – someone that does not know or follow the rules of the road. The earliest known reference to this is in 1905 Kansas, where drivers often disregard traffic rules and drive on the wrong side of the road. The term later migrated to those walking and ignoring the proper place to cross the road – hence jay-walker.

#597 The Dutch royal family sent 100,000 tulips to the city of Ottawa, Ontario, Canada, in 1945 as gratitude for sheltering future Queen Juliana and her family for the three years of Nazi occupation of the Netherlands during World War II. They currently send 20,000 tulips yearly to Ottawa. Because of the abundance and popularity of tulips, the Canadian Tulip Festival was organized in Ottawa in 1953 and has been held with over 650,000 visitors annually.

#598 The Carlton Tavern pub in London is the only building on its street to survive the German Blitzkrieg bombing during World War II. Due to its historical importance, it was considered for special protection in 2015. Shockingly, the company that owned the building demolished it during Easter weekend without permission, intending to build apartments above a newly constructed pub. Following the incident, the Westminster City Council mandated that the owner rebuild the pub precisely as it was before it was demolished. The pub has since reopened in April 2021.

Interesting Stories and Fascinating Facts   **More** than **Trivia**

History & Language

#599 The term "unfriend" has been around for centuries. Several of William Shakespeare's plays used the term unfriended to describe someone who lost their friend or friends.

#600 "The Muffin Man" is a classic English nursery rhyme that originated in the early 1800s. The rhyme tells the story of a vendor who goes door-to-door delivering freshly baked goods, particularly muffins. The muffins mentioned in the rhyme are typically known as English muffins and are different from the sweeter, cupcake-shaped muffins commonly found today.

#601 Though not the oldest culture in the United States, the Clovis culture in Clovis, New Mexico, dates back over 12,000 years. The Clovis people are the ancestors of about 80% of all living Native American populations in the Americas. One of the most remarkable discoveries of the Clovis culture was the Clovis point, a spear tip chipped from jasper, obsidian, or other brittle stone about four inches long and a third of an inch thick. More than 10,000 Clovis points have been discovered in 1,500 locations across North America.

#602 When referencing a year or a time of day, there is often an abbreviation after the number. When talking about years, there is BC or AD. BC is an abbreviation for "Before Christ," and AD is short for a Latin term, *anno Domini*, which means "In the year of our Lord." You may also see BCE instead of BC, which means "Before Current Era," and CE, which means "Current Era." When speaking of the time of day, there is AM (also A.M., am, a.m.) and PM (P.M., pm, p.m.). The abbreviation "AM" is short for *ante meridiem*, which is Latin for "before midday or noon," and "PM" is short for *post meridiem*, which is Latin for "post (after) midday or noon."

More than Trivia *Interesting Stories and Fascinating Facts*

History & Language

#603 The time in Ireland and England used to be defined by the sunrise and sunset. But a standardized time became necessary. Because the sun rose 25 minutes later in Dublin than in Greenwich, Ireland got their own time zone in 1880 called Dublin Mean Time (DMT). DMT lasted until 1916 when the House of Commons abolished Dublin Mean Time, and all of Britain adopted Greenwich Mean Time. Countess Markievicz, an Irish rebel leader, claimed Irish "public feeling (was) outraged by forcing of English time on us."

#604 *Gesundheit*, the German word for health, is the usual response to sneezing in Germany and often in the United States. Also common in the U.S. is "Bless you" or "God bless you." English translations for other responses are "Live for a long time" (Chechen), "To your health" (Latvian, Lithuanian, Macedonian, and others), "May God forgive you" (Mongolian), and "Live long, live good" (Turkish). In some cultures, such as Mandarin Chinese, Japanese, Korean, or Vietnamese, often nothing is said except to express concern ("Are you all right?").

#605 The State House bell, later dubbed the Liberty Bell, hangs outside Independence Hall in Philadelphia. Its biblical inscription, "Proclaim Liberty Throughout All the Land Unto All the Inhabitants thereof," has been a rallying call for liberty for several causes over the last 200+ years. So a national outcry was understandable when on April 1, 1996, Taco Bell announced they had purchased the Liberty Bell and changed its name to the Taco Liberty Bell. Angry phone calls flooded the Independence National Historical Park, and officials quickly called a press conference to deny that the bell had been sold. Taco Bell finally admitted that the sale of the bell was an April Fools' Day joke. Regardless of the outcry, company sales of tacos, enchiladas, and burritos rose by more than a half million dollars that week.

Interesting Stories and Fascinating Facts   **More** than **Trivia**

#606 Webster's New International Dictionary (second edition, 1934) mistakenly included the non-existent word "dord" as a synonym for "density" in physics and chemistry. The mistake occurred when the dictionary's chemistry editor sent a note intending to add "density" to an existing list of words that the letter "D" can abbreviate. The note he sent said: "D or d, cont./density," and the phrase "D or d" was interpreted as a single word and included in the publication. An editor discovered the error in 1939; subsequent dictionary editions removed "dord" starting in 1940. It was entirely removed by 1947.

Chapter 15

Health & Medical

#607 It is estimated that between 6.7 million and 20 million Americans have hoarding disorder. There is an International OCD Foundation to help those affected by this disorder.

#608 Scientists in Japan have discovered that the human body emits a faint light that is not visible to the naked eye. The amount of glow changes during the day, and the face glows more than the rest of the body.

#609 Finnish researchers suggest that spending at least five hours each month in nature can help reduce the risk of depression, alcoholism, and suicide. This practice, also known as "Nature therapy," "Forest therapy," or *shinrin-yoku* in Japan, where it is supported by the state. While the exact reasons for the positive effects of nature therapy are not fully understood, it is known to have health benefits. Additionally, the "Profile of Mood States" psychological rating test has shown a correlation between forest therapy and physiological benefits.

Health & Medical

#610 Some people can hear their eyeballs moving in their sockets, saying it sounds like sandpaper on wood. This is a symptom of "Superior canal dehiscence syndrome" (SCDS). It is a rare condition of the inner ear that can cause sound distortion and balance problems. About 1% - 2% of people have SCDS.

#611 A study by the University of California, San Diego, found that the average person generates about 14 ounces of poop daily, which works out to 6 lbs. per week and 320 lbs. per year. The average life expectancy for men is 76 and 81 for women, which is 24,329 lbs. of poop for men and 25,920 lbs. for women produced in a lifetime.

#612 We have goosebumps because a tiny muscle surrounds the root of every hair on our body, and when the muscle tightens, a small bump appears on our skin. These small muscles can tighten when we get cold or have intense feelings of any kind. This same reflex causes the hair to stand up on the back of a cat or dog when it gets surprised or experiences fear.

#613 Highway hypnosis is when you zone out while driving and cannot remember the last few miles of your trip. It is not drowsy driving as much as it is distracted driving. Like riding a bike, you are on autopilot with your mind thinking about something else besides the driving details and your surroundings. This can reduce your reaction time and increase the possibility of an accident. Highway hypnosis happens because of a lack of mental stimulation, such as monotonous scenery. To avoid this, experts say to consciously notice things around you - road signs, other vehicles, and scenery. Other tips include rolling down the window, turning off cruise control, talking to yourself, and playing loud, upbeat music.

More than Trivia   *Interesting Stories and Fascinating Facts*

Health & Medical

#614 "Phantom Vibration Syndrome" is when you think your mobile phone is vibrating due to an incoming call, and it is not. Some have developed the habit of detecting an incoming call so much that a slight muscle twitch or a movement of their clothes makes them think their phone is vibrating. Before being called phantom vibration syndrome, the condition was called "ringxiety."

#615 The hardest substance in the human body is not bone but tooth enamel. On the Mohs scale of mineral hardness, tooth enamel, at a hardness of 5, is between ordinary steel (at 4-4.5) and concrete and granite (at 6-7). Not only is enamel hard, but it is also elastic enough to withstand many years of chewing. Scientists have tried to create artificial enamel for years because the body cannot regenerate it. They have made strides but have yet to create a product viable enough for the dentist's office.

#616 The antics of circus clowns are fun to watch for most people, but almost 8% of Americans have coulrophobia, the fear of clowns. Stephen King has triskaidekaphobia (fear of the number 13), Oprah Winfrey has globophobia (fear of balloons,) and Alfred Hitchcock had ovophobia (fear of eggs.) Some common phobias that people have are arachnophobia (fear of spiders), mysophobia (fear of germs), astraphobia (fear of thunder and lightning), aerophobia (fear of flying), acrophobia (fear of heights), ophidiophobia (fear of snakes), and claustrophobia (fear of confined spaces). But there are also some unusual phobias, such as bibliophobia (fear of books), cherophobia (fear of happiness), gamophobia (fear of marriage), koumpounophobia (fear of buttons on clothing), pogonophobia (fear of beards), and anthophobia (fear of the color yellow).

Interesting Stories and Fascinating Facts **More than Trivia**

Health & Medical

#617 Spider webs were used in ancient Greece and Rome to help heal wounds. Spider webs are rich in vitamin K, which aids in blood clotting. Shakespeare mentioned their medical use in his play *A Midsummer Night's Dream*.

#618 You gain almost 1/2 inch in height while you sleep at night. This is because you are not affected by gravity as you sleep, and your body replenishes lost fluids between the discs in your spine, which stretch and relax. NASA astronauts gain up to two inches in height when they are on missions, free from the force of earth's gravity.

More than Trivia   *Interesting Stories and Fascinating Facts*

Chapter 16

Science & Engineering

#619 In the 1800s, before electricity was available to light indoor and outdoor stages, a method called "limelight" was used. This involved heating quicklime (calcium oxide) to produce a bright light, which gave rise to the phrase "in the limelight."

#620 Carrots have a high water content, but they stay rigid and crunchy because of the cellulose they contain. Researchers in Britain have discovered that using this cellulose in mixing concrete increases the strength of concrete by 80% and prevents cracking. And it creates a more eco-friendly product.

#621 In 2011, while searching for a cure for AIDS, scientists at the Mayo Clinic created glow-in-the-dark cats. The scientists were studying cats because there is a disease that affects cats called FIV (Feline Immunodeficiency Virus), similar to HIV in humans. They injected two genes into the cats, one containing a fluorescent protein from a jellyfish. If the cat's fur shone yellow-green in the dark, they knew the experiment worked.

Interesting Stories and Fascinating Facts **More** than **Trivia**

Science & Engineering

#622 NASA gave Stanford engineer Thomas R. Kane a $60,000 research grant in the 1960s to study falling cats to help astronauts orient and move their bodies in zero gravity. In this falling cat phenomenon, cats can turn their bodies in mid-air after being dropped belly up to land on their feet.

#623 Early roller coasters had perfectly circular loops, which caused pain to their riders. This loop type could cause extreme G-force spikes exceeding those that a fighter pilot or astronaut experiences. Most roller coasters shut down until the 1970s when a new inverted teardrop design was created that gave riders all the excitement without the pain.

#624 The Danyang-Kunshan Grand Bridge in China, 102 miles long, is the longest bridge in the world and is part of the Beijing-Shanghai High-Speed Railway line. The bridge took 4 years to build, being completed in 2010. It is built to withstand typhoons and an 8-magnitude earthquake. China also has other long bridges, including the 72-mile Cangde Grand Bridge, the 70-mile Tianjin Grand Bridge, the 49-mile Weinan Weihe Grand Bridge, the 30-mile-long Beijing Grand Bridge, and others.

#625 Lab-grown, or synthetic, diamonds are becoming more popular and less expensive to create. Lab-grown diamonds can be made in under four weeks and are chemically, physically, and optically identical to a natural, mined diamond. A tiny diamond slice is needed to begin the process, which includes high temperatures and pressure, much like a naturally mined diamond needs. China is the world's largest producer of lab-grown diamonds producing over half of them, with India and the United States in a distant 2nd and 3rd place, each producing about 15% of them.

More than Trivia   *Interesting Stories and Fascinating Facts*

Science & Engineering

#626 Researchers at the University of Kitakyushu in Japan say used disposable diapers need not end up in a landfill. Once the diapers are washed, dried, and shredded, they can replace up to 40% of the sand used in concrete production. Although there are obstacles to overcome, a prototype home has been constructed in Indonesia to demonstrate the feasibility of this innovative process.

#627 A properly built igloo can create a temperature difference of up to 100 degrees (F) between the inside and outside using just body heat. This is because igloos work similarly to a blanket by trapping body heat and preventing it from escaping. Hardened, compressed snow blocks from the ground are used instead of freshly fallen snow. Snow is a great insulator due to its high air content, which helps to retain heat. The interior of the igloo is built in a stairstep pattern. The highest level is reserved for sleeping since warm air tends to rise, while the lower level serves as an entrance and storage area.

#628 The directors of the 1893 World's Fair in Chicago challenged American engineers to create a monument surpassing the Eiffel Tower, which was built for the previous World's Fair in 1889 Paris. Civil engineer George Washington Gale Ferris accepted the challenge and proposed building a rotating wheel from which visitors could view the entire fair from the air. Original safety concerns were overcome, and construction was begun on the $400,000 "Ferris Wheel." There were 36 cars in the wheel, each with 40 revolving chairs, accommodating up to 60 people for a total capacity of 2,160. The wheel carried 38,000 passengers daily, taking 20 minutes to complete two revolutions. The cost to ride the Ferris Wheel was 50 cents.

Interesting Stories and Fascinating Facts **More** than **Trivia**

Science & Engineering

#629 Rotary ceiling fans in the 1860s were powered by a stream of running water in conjunction with a turbine to drive a system of belts that turned the two-blade fan units.

#630 As the population of the Roman Empire grew, they needed more water than the local streams and wells could provide. To address this need, the Romans built aqueducts. An aqueduct is simply a means to transport water from a remote source, typically by gravity, using a ditch, canal, or system of pipes. The first aqueduct they built was the Aqua Appia aqueduct in 312 BC. The Aqua Appia was a 10-mile-long, mostly underground channel with a 30-foot drop over its length. Over nearly 540 years, the Romans constructed 11 aqueducts to supply water to their population of over 1 million citizens. The term aqueduct comes from the Latin words *aqua* (water) and *ductus* (led or guided).

#631 Though many people use refrigerator magnets to hold pictures on the front of their refrigerator, you wouldn't dare use a rare-earth magnet as it is much too strong. Some larger ones are marketed as fishing magnets that people lower into a lake with a rope to find metal objects under the water. A 3-pound rare-earth, or Neodymium magnet, can have a 1,000-pound pulling force. Rare-earth magnets are common but expensive and difficult to extract from the earth. China controls more than 80% of the market. The U.S. and other countries are trying to catch up, but it will take years. An exciting new development, however, is that scientists have discovered a way to create a rare-earth magnet alternative made from a material found only previously in meteorites. The compound is called tetrataenite, and though a commercially viable process to make it in the lab is years away, the discovery could disrupt the rare-earth market worldwide.

More than Trivia   *Interesting Stories and Fascinating Facts*

Science & Engineering

#632 NASA uses urine and sweat to make drinking water on the International Space Station far superior to what municipal water systems produce on Earth. With new equipment and processes, they can now recover and recycle 98% of the water on board, currently in urine, sweat, and even the humidity of a crew member's breath. This significant achievement allows more scientific equipment to be sent to the station and less water than before.

#633 By 400 BC, Persian engineers had built a structure called a *yakhchal* where they could make and store ice in the desert. The yakhchal (meaning ice pit) was a dome structure about 60 feet tall and containing about 180,000 cubic feet of storage space below the surface. The yakhchal worked well because of its aerodynamic design and the insulating material used on the walls. The mortar on the walls was a specific mixture of clay, sand, lime, egg whites, ash, and goat hair. The yakhchal was accessible to everyone in society, whether a commoner or royalty, and some of the structures are still standing today.

#634 The iconic roadway, Route 66, from Chicago, Illinois, to Santa Monica, California, has a quarter-mile stretch in New Mexico that plays music when you drive over it. To hear the music, you must travel east from Albuquerque towards Tijeras between mile markers 4 and 5 at exactly 45 MPH. The music you hear is "America the Beautiful." The New Mexico Department of Transportation accomplished this engineering feat in 2014 by placing rumble strips at a precise distance from one another on the road. This method causes your tires to vibrate at specific frequencies to produce the notes of the song, just like the vibrations of a guitar string at a specific frequency create the sound of a particular note.

Interesting Stories and Fascinating Facts **More** than **Trivia**

#635 Water towers are elevated water storage tanks that primarily rely on gravity to supply water where needed. Water towers vary, but a standard height is about 130 feet. Every foot in elevation will produce about .43 pounds per square inch (PSI) of water pressure, so a one-hundred-foot tall water tower will provide about 43 PSI. Because they work by gravity, water towers can supply water for a limited period during a power outage. A pump typically replenishes the water in a water tower during off-peak hours.

#636 The "Ig Nobel Prize" is a parody of the Nobel Prize awards that highlights ten unusual or trivial scientific achievements each year to make people laugh and think. As of 2021, Sir Andre Geim is the only person to have received both an Ig Nobel Prize and a Nobel Prize. He won his Ig Nobel Prize in 2000 for using magnetism to levitate a frog. He then later received a Nobel Prize in 2010 for his groundbreaking work on the electromagnetic properties of graphene. Although some view the Ig Nobel Prizes as a critique of seemingly trivial research, it's important to note that such research has led to some significant breakthroughs.

#637 Isaac Newton discovered that things do not have color in themselves. In other words, roses are not red, and violets are not blue. Color is a property of light; all possible colors are contained in white sunlight and have their own "wavelength." When light strikes an object, such as an orange, the orange absorbs all of the colors in the light except for orange, which it reflects, and that is the color we perceive it to be. We perceive color because we have millions of cells in the retina of our eye called "cones" that are sensitive to the millions of different colors available. The appropriate cones sense the particular color of light and notify the brain what that color is and that is what we "see."

More than Trivia   *Interesting Stories and Fascinating Facts*

Science & Engineering

#638 Fireworks are explosions of numerous small pellets of black powder called stars. The main ingredient in fireworks is black powder, which explodes when lit on fire. In addition to black powder, firework stars contain different chemicals or metals to create specific colors. The stars are intentionally arranged to create various firework shapes or images. The fireworks we enjoy are developed by trained professionals called pyrotechnicians. They make precise calculations to ensure that each firework reaches the correct altitude and explodes at the right time and location. Designing, preparing, and setting up a 20-minute show can take several days to weeks.

More than Trivia   *Interesting Stories and Fascinating Facts*

Chapter 17

Travel & Transportation

#639 Cruise ships have morgues in case of the unfortunate death of a passenger. The morgue is generally in the lowest part of the ship in a discrete location. It can typically accommodate 3 to 6 bodies.

#640 Japan is developing a magnetic levitation railway system called Chuo Shinkansen to link Tokyo to Osaka. The technology is called SCMaglev (superconducting magnetic levitation). Once the train reaches 93 mph, it creates a magnetic field that lifts the train 4 inches above the guideway. On a test track in 2015, the train reached 375 mph with a manned seven-car system. The initial construction will connect Tokyo to Nagoya in 40 minutes (178 miles) and, eventually, Tokyo to Osaka in 67 minutes (272 miles). Most of the track will run through tunnels under the Japanese Alps, some as deep as 130 feet. The train will travel at a maximum speed of 314 mph. The first link to Nagoya is expected to be completed in 2027, and the Osaka section around 2037. The estimated cost for the project in 2011 was almost $67 trillion.

Travel & Transportation

#641 Britain's first speeding ticket was issued to Walter Arnold in 1896 for driving a horseless carriage at 8 MPH (4 times the legal limit). He was chased and pulled over by a police constable on a bicycle. Later that year, the speed limit was increased to 14 MPH.

#642 The distance between the inside edges of a train track is called its track gauge, and the standard track gauge is 4 ft 8 1/2 in (1,435 mm). That is used on about 60% of the railroad tracks in the world. High-speed railways use the standard track gauge; anything wider than that is not necessarily faster, nor does it carry more weight. In the early days of the railways, some countries feared being invaded by other countries, so they intentionally used a different track gauge. Some say this unusual track gauge dates back to the days of Roman Chariots and the ruts they made in the ground, but this cannot be confirmed.

#643 In 1958, two pilots, Robert Timm, and John Wayne Cook, flew a single-engine Cessna 172 from Las Vegas, Nevada, and continued flying for 64 days straight without landing. This incredible feat set a new world record for flight endurance. Their journey took them mainly over the deserts around Las Vegas. They covered approximately 150,000 miles, equivalent to traveling around the earth six times. A former World War II bomber pilot, Timm worked as a slot machine mechanic. To increase the plane's fuel capacity, they installed a 95-gallon belly tank in addition to the 47 gallons carried in the wings. They also modified the oil lines to change the oil and filters without turning off the engine. Twice a day, they received fresh fuel from a truck with a fuel tank and pump while flying over a closed, straight stretch of highway approximately 20 feet off the ground. They used an electric winch to lower a hook and retrieve the refueling hose, which took about 3 minutes to fill. They refueled 128 times throughout their journey.

More than Trivia *Interesting Stories and Fascinating Facts*

Travel & Transportation

#644 *Air Horse One* is a specially designed Boeing 727 airplane for transporting horses to and from popular horse racing destinations. They can fly up to twenty-one thoroughbreds at a time along with their entourages. Most horses do well with flying, and the plane takes extra measures to ensure a smooth flight. Oh yes, and light snacks of hay and water are offered.

#645 In 1888, Bertha Benz, the wife of automobile inventor Carl Benz, became the first person to drive a car over a long distance (65 miles). Though her husband had not marketed his invention, she wanted to show that the car would be useful to the general public. She had to make several repairs and adjustments during her trip with her two teenage sons. When the wooden brakes began to fail, she visited a cobbler to install leather brake linings. Her sons had to push the car up steep roads, so she suggested adding a third gear for climbing hills. Her trip received significant attention, and Bertha's suggestions became vital to the future development of automobiles.

#646 Fred and August Duesenberg founded the Duesenberg Automobile & Motors Company in 1920. They were said to be the most luxurious American cars ever made. In addition to passenger cars, they made racing cars and won the 1921 French Grand Prix, the first American car to do so. They also won the Indianapolis 500 four times during the 1920s. The body and cabin of their Model Js were custom-built. Two modified Model Js, the SSJ, were made for actors Gary Cooper and Clark Gable in 1935. Cooper's car was sold at auction in 2018 for $22 million. The company was sold and dissolved in 1937. There were several attempts to revive the vehicle, including the Duesenberg II, which had updates like air conditioning and automatic transmission. But that factory closed in 2001.

Interesting Stories and Fascinating Facts   **More** than **Trivia**

Travel & Transportation

#647 Modern roundabouts were first standardized in the UK in 1966, and the first one built in the U.S. was in Nevada in 1990. They are generally met with resistance before construction but are favored when drivers gain experience with them.

#648 From 1924-1954, the **STOP** sign was yellow with black letters. Though traffic stop lights dating back to 1912 were red, the red dye color used for signs would fade over time. However, in 1954, sign makers started using fade-resistant porcelain enamel to prevent fading. That year, the Joint Committee on Uniform Traffic Control Devices mandated that all stop signs be red with white letters, which has been the standard since then. Before 1924, there were no federal regulations governing stop signs, so it wasn't unusual to see square signs made of metal or wood with black letters on a white background. Also, because of the steel shortage during World War II, many signs were made with wood, which was repainted as they faded.

#649 Owning long-term or permanent residential quarters on a cruise ship that sails around the world is an expensive but possible dream for some. One of the least expensive options is on the MV *Narrative* with 11 different accommodations, from a 270-square-foot apartment for about $1 million to a two-story, four-bedroom, 1,970-square foot townhome for about $8 million. And that doesn't include monthly living fees starting at around $2,100 per person. Other permanent cruise ship options are *The World* ($2 Million - $1 Million), the MS *Dark Island* ($10.7 Million - $140 Million +), and others. They typically have all the comforts of home and then some for those accustomed to a more luxurious lifestyle. These cruise ships typically circumnavigate the globe about every three years, stopping at various ports for 2-3 days at a time. These floating residences may sound expensive, but they have no problem selling them.

More than **Trivia**   *Interesting Stories and Fascinating Facts*

Travel & Transportation

#650 The Trans-Siberian Railway is the longest railway line in the world, covering over 5,700 miles through Russia. It goes through eight time zones and takes eight days to ride the entire length. Expansion projects are underway to connect it to Mongolia, China, and North Korea, and there are proposals to expand it to Tokyo, Japan.

#651 One of the earliest electric vehicles was the Belgian *La Jamais Contente* (The Never Contented) which established a land speed record of 62 mph in 1899. The torpedo-shaped vehicle had Michelin tires and two 25kW motors that ran off batteries. The driver, Camille Jenatzy, was nicknamed *Le Diable Rouge* (The Red Devil) for the color of his beard.

#652 The *Shania Train* is a new luxury Swiss train named after performer Shania Twain. The musician has lived in Lake Geneva, Switzerland, for ten years, and the new Golden Pass Express train, *Shania Train*, connects a popular tourist route from Montreux on Lake Geneva to Interlaken in the Swiss Alps. Unique to this train is its ability to adapt to different track widths (gauges) along the journey and the variance of car body heights to accommodate the various tracks it travels on.

#653 When the U.S. President or other heads of state need transportation, they use heavily modified vehicles. Sometimes, heads of state will bring cars manufactured in their home country when visiting foreign lands. The American President uses a modified Cadillac, while the British monarch typically uses a Rolls-Royce or Bentley and sometimes a Range Rover. Saudi Arabia opts for a Mercedes S-600; other countries, such as Russia, also use some Mercedes models. Japan uses a special G51 Toyota Century Royal limousine, while Sweden primarily uses Volvo and occasionally Saab.

Interesting Stories and Fascinating Facts **More** than **Trivia**

Travel & Transportation

Chapter 18

Tech

#654 The first TV remote in 1950, dubbed "Lazy Bones," was linked to the TV set by a long wire. In 1956 a wireless remote was developed called "Zenith Space Command."

#655 One of the experimental pointing devices developed for a 1960s computer was a head-mounted device attached to the chin or nose. Fortunately, the mouse won out.

#656 That mysterious # symbol on your keyboard or phone is technically called an OCTOTHORPE. That little fellow is known as the pound, number, or hashtag. The origin of the name is not certain, but one version is certainly interesting. Don MacPherson, a supervisor at Bell Labs, created the made-up word Octothorpe to describe the # symbol on the new telephones with their keypads being put in place to replace the rotary dial phone system. "OCTO" is for the eight points of the symbol, and "THORPE" is in honor of Jim Thorpe, the all-around athlete stripped of the two gold medals he won in the 1912 Summer Olympics. Don MacPherson was part of a group trying to get Thorpe's Olympic medals returned.

Tech

#657 The barcode was patented in the U.S. in 1951 and was based on Morse code. The barcode became commercially successful when it was used to automate supermarket checkout systems in the 1970s.

#658 In 1994, Microsoft designers asked musician/producer/visual artist Brian Eno to create a musical piece used as the start-up sound for the Windows 95 operating system. They wanted it to be inspiring, optimistic, emotional, futuristic, and only 3 1/4 seconds long. The sound became known as the "Microsoft Sound." He created the sound on an Apple Macintosh computer and stated later, "I've never used a PC in my life; I don't like them."

#659 Sony released 700,000 Night Vision camcorders in 1998 that could see through people's clothes. When Sony learned their camcorders had a form of X-Ray vision, they immediately recalled them, but not before some inappropriate photos appeared on the Internet that was taken with the camcorder. The camcorders had a lens that used Infrared Rays (IR) to take pictures in the dark. However, when used in the daytime, this special lens could see through dark clothing, thin fabrics, and swimsuits. Whoops!

#660 The world's first website was created on August 6, 1991, and is still up and running. It was built and hosted on a NeXT computer by the inventor of the World Wide Web (W3), British scientist Tim Berners-Lee. It was initially created for information sharing between scientists around the world. The World Wide Web wasn't very popular until 1993, with the release of Mosaic, a web browser. You can view the world's first website at http://info.cern.ch/hypertext/WWW/TheProject.html. There are no images, just text, and links about the World Wide Web.

More than Trivia   *Interesting Stories and Fascinating Facts*

Tech

#661 Apple's Macintosh computer line was named after the McIntosh apple, a popular apple in Eastern Canada and New England. Jef Raskin, the Apple employee that named the Macintosh computer changed the spelling to avoid conflict with McIntosh Laboratory, the high-end audio equipment manufacturer in Binghampton, New York.

#662 In 1971, Ray Tomlinson created the first email program and randomly chose the @ symbol on the keyboard to separate the user name from the machine's domain name. It was among the least-used characters on the keyboard and in software programs, so it would not be easily confused as having a different meaning. In the U.S., the @ symbol is called the "at" symbol, but it has different meanings in other countries. It is called "monkey's tail" in South Africa, Germany, and the Netherlands. In the Czech Republic, it means "pickled herring." The Danish and Swedish terms mean "elephant's trunk."

#663 Though many know of Steve Jobs and Steve Wozniak as the founders of Apple Computer, few know there was a third founder named Ronald Wayne. In the initial partnership agreement, Jobs and Wozniak owned a 45% stake in the company, and Wayne had a 10% stake. As Wayne was 21 years older than Jobs and 16 years older than Wozniak, he was "the adult in the room," hired to arbitrate any disputes between the other two and provide guidance for the business venture. Wayne made several significant contributions to Apple, including establishing the proprietary nature of Apple computers compared to the open-source architecture of PCs. However, because of Wayne's previous business experience and risk aversion, he withdrew from the partnership less than two weeks after it started. He sold his partnership back for $800 and received a final payment of $1,500 to forfeit any future claims he may have against Apple.

Interesting Stories and Fascinating Facts **More than Trivia**

#664 The word "Android" is a gender-specific term meaning a mobile robot with a male human form. A female robot or android is called a "gynoid."

#665 Russell Kirsch, who invented the pixel in 1957, later expressed regret that he made the pixel a square shape. Pixels are the digital dots used to produce images on a computer or phone screen. Kirsch later developed a way to create pixels with variable shapes, but the idea never caught on.

#666 Popular website domains are .com, .org, and .gov. There are many others, including .tv, an Internet country code for Tuvalu, a group of islands in the Pacific Ocean located about halfway between Australia and Hawaii. About 10% of Tuvalu's revenue comes from the royalties of the .tv domain name.

#667 Some websites use a CAPTCHA form to prevent website spammers or bots from accessing a website. The CAPTCHA form requires you to enter the correct characters that are shown as a distorted display of characters you see on the website. CAPTCHA is an acronym for "Completely Automated Public Turing test to tell Computers and Humans Apart."

#668 In the UK in 2010, there was a race between a carrier pigeon and rural broadband to see who delivered information the fastest. The pigeon won. Ten pigeons with attached USB drives were released at the same time a upload of a five-minute video began. The pigeons completed their 75-mile journey, while only 24% of the files were uploaded. A similar race was done the year before with similar results. That race featured Winston, the carrier pigeon who has his own Facebook page with 5,000 followers.

More than Trivia *Interesting Stories and Fascinating Facts*

#669 One of the first handheld calculators was the Sharp EL-8. It came out in January 1971, weighed about a pound and a half, and cost $395.

#670 The first "smartphone" was the IBM Simon, a touchscreen PDA first marketed in 1994. The Apple iPhone came along in January 2007, the Samsung Galaxy S4 Zoom in 2013, and the Google Pixel in 2016.

#671 In 1950, the Canadian National Exhibition featured Bertie the Brain, a 13-foot-tall game computer that played tic-tac-toe with anyone who wanted to challenge it. It was one of the earliest game computers ever built.

#672 The Global Positioning System (GPS) is owned by the U.S. government and financed through the Department of Defense to the tune of about $2 billion per year. It comprises a minimum of 24 satellites, and at any time, a minimum of 6 will be in view to users anywhere in the world. Four or more satellites are required for regular operation. Positioning accuracy varies depending on the receiver, signal blockage, and the satellites used. Accuracy can be as less than an inch and up to 16 feet.

#673 When you see an ad for an Apple iPhone or iPad, the displayed time is always 9:41. Apple always plans the big product reveals to happen about 40 minutes into their keynote presentations. Then when the product image appears on the big screen, the time on it will closely match the time on the audience's watches. Apple initially used 9:42 for the time because that is when Steve Jobs announced the first iPhone in 2007, and that is what the product image showed on the big screen behind him as he said, "Today, Apple is going to reinvent the phone." Apple later adjusted the time displayed to 9:41.

Interesting Stories and Fascinating Facts   ***More* than Trivia**

#674   In 2005, Sony/BMG distributed 22 million music CDs that installed hidden spyware on the user's computer to collect and send information about their listening habits back to Sony. The spyware could not be easily removed, creating vulnerabilities that malware could exploit. The spyware installed was XCP (Extended Copy Protection) for Windows PCs and Mediamax on Macs. Over 80 album titles were shipped, including those by Celine Dion, Jennifer Lopez, Ray Charles, Patty Loveless, Britney Spears, Sarah McLachlan, Santana, Foo Fighters, Dave Matthews Band, and Alicia Keys. This effort by Sony was to protect their intellectual property from online file-sharing networks such as Napster and others. NPR was one of the early reporters of this copy protection rootkit issue, and Sony faced multiple lawsuits.

Chapter 19

Plants & Animals

#675 The squirrel is one of the top causes of power outages in the U.S., causing 10%-20% of power outages yearly.

#676 The bird often referred to as a peacock is actually a peafowl. Peacock is the term for the male of the species, while the female is a peahen.

#677 Though a pumpkin farmer in Italy holds the world record for heaviest pumpkin at 2,702 pounds, a grower in Clarence, New York, recently claimed the record for the heaviest pumpkin grown in the U.S. with his 2,554-pound behemoth.

#678 There is a jellyfish, *Turritopsis dohrnii*, commonly known as the immortal jellyfish, that can effectively live forever. It can do this through a cell development process called transdifferentiation, which alters their cells and transforms them into new types of cells. However, most of them are killed by predators or succumb to a disease before they can change their cells.

Interesting Stories and Fascinating Facts   **More** than **Trivia**

Plants & Animals

#679 The top Ten most popular pet names are 1. Max 2. Sam 3. Lady 4. Bear 5. Smokey 6. Shadow 7. Kitty 8. Molly 9. Buddy 10. Brandy.

#680 When a possum is threatened or harmed, it will faint and appear dead. It is not pretending to be dead – it has an involuntary physiological response where it loses consciousness for a few minutes to a few hours. It foams at the mouth during this time, and a foul-smelling fluid is secreted from the anal glands. During this time, it can be prodded, turned over, or even carried away without a reaction.

#681 Cows cannot really jump over the moon, as the nursery rhyme says, but they can jump 4-5 feet high on average. That's good for an animal that weighs between 800 and 1,400 pounds. Compare that to an elephant weighing 8,000 pounds on average, which cannot jump at all. Surprisingly though, an elephant can run 10 to 15 miles per hour, and if you have seen some of the old *Tarzan* movies, you know they can run pretty fast.

#682 The sperm whale is so named because of *spermaceti*, a liquid mixture in the whale's head, initially mistaken for sperm. There are about 500 gallons of spermaceti in the whale's head that helps in echolocation, a sonar system the whale uses for navigation and hunting. The sperm whale is the largest of toothed whales, with the male reaching over 70 feet in length and weighing up to 55 tons. Their diet is typically squid, but they also eat sharks, rays, and octopuses. The sperm whale was Captain Ahab's object of pursuit in Herman Melville's 1851 novel *Moby-Dick*. Melville associated the Bible's Leviathan with the sperm whale. One unique behavior of the sperm whale is that they sleep vertically, usually head up, just below the water's surface, in pods of 5 or 6 whales.

More than Trivia   *Interesting Stories and Fascinating Facts*

Plants & Animals

#683 The construction of a cat's eye allows it to take in more light and to see six times better than a human in low-light conditions. It cannot see in complete darkness, but in most situations, there is enough light for a cat to see well. It has better peripheral vision than a human, but its distance vision is not as good. Some say that a cat's color vision is limited to blues and grays, whereas a human has excellent and vibrant color vision.

#684 J. Fred Muggs is a chimpanzee who was a TV personality from 1953 to 1975. He appeared on several TV shows, including *The Today Show*. His wardrobe consisted of 450 outfits. Mr. Muggs was also an artist, and in 1958, one of his finger paintings was used as the cover of *Mad* magazine #38. *TV Guide* had an annual feature called "The J. Fred Muggs Awards for Distinguished Foolishness," which highlighted some of the year's most questionable TV programs or episodes.

#685 Albatrosses are among the largest flying birds, with the *Diomedia* (great albatross) having a wingspan of up to 12 feet. The albatross can fly for years without touching down on land and can travel thousands of miles. However, they land on the water to feed and only touch the ground to breed and care for their young. They seldom flap their wings while in flight and can lock them when fully extended, which involves little exertion for the outstretched wings. It is unknown if the albatross takes power naps for a few seconds while they fly, as some birds do. Some believe that the albatross stops at night to sleep on the water. They can live for decades, with some surpassing 60 years. The albatross has a complicated mating dance that can take years for the males to learn all the steps. If the male doesn't properly impress the female, she can be picky and move on to the next suitor.

Interesting Stories and Fascinating Facts **More than Trivia**

Plants & Animals

#686 The armadillo is an amazing creature. They can hold their breath for six minutes or more and jump straight upward, about three to four feet in the air when startled.

#687 An albino bottlenose dolphin was discovered in Calcasieu Lake, Louisiana, in 2007. She is pinkish in color and has been named Pinky. She was photographed in 2015, and a video of two albino dolphins was taken in 2017, presumably of Pinky and her baby.

#688 When Leona Helmsley, a real estate investor in Connecticut, died in 2007, she left her Maltese dog "Trouble," a $12 million trust fund, which a judge later reduced to $2 million. One of the wealthiest cat heirs ever was "Blackie", a UK cat that was left $12.5 million when his antique dealer owner, Ben Rea, died in 1988.

#689 The smallest flower in the world is the size of a candy sprinkle, weighing as much as two grains of salt. It is called a Wolffia flower, or watermeal, and you can fit about 5,000 into a thimble. They are found in quiet freshwater lakes or marshes worldwide, and because they have no roots, they often float on the surface of the water, where they resemble cornmeal. It produces the world's smallest fruit and is eaten as a vegetable in Asia.

#690 One of the most popular attractions at the 1904 World's Fair in St. Louis was Beautiful Jim Key, a performing horse that some called the "World's Smartest Horse." Owned and trained by "Dr." William Key, a former slave and self-taught veterinarian, the horse could spell his name using alphabet blocks and do simple arithmetic. His gravesite is in a field behind a private residence near Shelbyville, Tennessee, and the site promotes kindness to animals and is free to visit.

More than Trivia   *Interesting Stories and Fascinating Facts*

Plants & Animals

#691 In 1876, the Belgian Society for the Elevation of the Domestic Cat devised a plan to use cats for mail delivery in and around Liege, Belgium. They equipped 37 cats with waterproof bags around their necks to carry out this task. However, if you know cats, you know this plan was far from purr-fect. In fact, the Kitty Mail Service was a terrible idea, and the plan was quickly scratched.

#692 Honey bees depend on both nectar and pollen for their survival. Nectar provides them with energy, and any surplus is stored in their stomach before being transferred to hive bees for further processing into honey. While collecting nectar, bees unintentionally pick up pollen from the male part of a flower called the stamen, which adheres to their legs. As bees move from one flower to another, the female part of the flower, known as the stigma, collects pollen from the bees. This process is how pollination occurs, enabling the plant to reproduce. In addition, the pollen that bees collect serves as a protein source for them, which they use to nourish their larvae.

#693 Ambergris, also known as liquid gold, originates in the sperm whale's digestive system and is expelled by vomiting or passed like fecal matter. It is found floating in the ocean or on shore. Ambergris is rare and expensive, and because the sperm whale is an endangered creature, the possession and trade of ambergris is prohibited in the United States and other places. Because of its cost and legal issues, a synthetic compound called ambroxide is often used in its place. When ambergris is first produced, it has an unpleasant odor, but as it ages, it becomes a pleasant musky scent. Perfume makers have used ambergris because it allows the fragrance to last longer. Ambergris has also been used to flavor foods, and in some cultures, it is considered an aphrodisiac.

Interesting Stories and Fascinating Facts **More** than **Trivia**

Plants & Animals

#694 The elephant's trunk can lift over 700 pounds, hold over 2 gallons of water, and crack a peanut shell without breaking the seed.

#695 The sloth feeds only on plants. Though they have a slow digestive system that produces gas, they don't fart. They absorb the gas into their bloodstream, releasing it through their mouths.

#696 Many cultures consider ladybirds (ladybugs) lucky and have nursery rhymes or local names that reflect this. One popular nursery rhyme from the early 19th century began "Ladybird Ladybird."

#697 In March 1846, an Egyptian snail believed to be dead was attached to an index card with glue at the British Museum. However, Museum officials discovered it alive in March 1850 when they transferred it to a glass jar, where it lived for another two years.

#698 Saving the Pufflings is a pastime for many children on the island of Heimaey off the southern coast of Iceland. Pufflings are baby Puffins that belong to three species, with Atlantic Puffins being the most common seabirds in Iceland. When they first leave their nest, they head to the ocean, where they spend the next 2-3 years before returning home. But when the Pufflings first leave their home, they are sometimes confused by the city lights, fly in the wrong direction, and wind up in town, where they need the children's help. On land, they struggle to take off for flight. The children search them out and rescue them from underneath parked cars and other dangerous locations. They then carry them to the ocean's edge and release them into the air, allowing them to start flying again and continue their journey.

More than Trivia   *Interesting Stories and Fascinating Facts*

Plants & Animals

#699 Hotel Hog Farms in China are a reality. There are several in operation but the largest is a 26-story high-rise breeding site in the southeast China city of Hubei, owned by Zhongxinkaiwei Modern Farming.

#700 Snails and slugs are slow because of their method of movement. They have a muscle band that runs along the underside of their body covered in mucus. Compressing this muscle compresses the sticky mucus on its underside into a slippery liquid so that it can glide over the ground or climb plants. When moving, they are limited by the number of muscle contractions and the amount of mucus they can produce.

#701 Cat Island, or Tashirojima, is a small island off the Oshika Peninsula in Japan. In 2015, the human population was about 80, while the cat population numbered hundreds. Around 1600, much of the island raised silkworms for their textiles, and Island residents kept cats to chase the mice away from their silkworms. Thousands of people, many of which are tourists, visit Tashirojima every year to see the cats. In Japanese culture, many believe cats bring good luck, including money and good fortune, to those who cross their path.

#702 The taste buds of a butterfly are on its feet and sometimes extend up its leg. Once they determine what they landed on is a good food source, they use their mouth, called the proboscis, to suck up the food like a straw. Butterflies don't have a tongue. The proboscis (mouth) is a long thin tube usually folded under the body and is unfolded as needed. Locating a good food source with their feet also helps the mother butterfly find a suitable plant to lay its eggs. When the caterpillars hatch from the eggs, they need to start eating right away, and being on a plant that is a good food source is vital.

Interesting Stories and Fascinating Facts **More** than **Trivia**

Plants & Animals

#703 In years past, there was an unfounded misconception that the bumblebee should not be able to fly based on its wings and body shape. As it turns out, the humble bumblebee can fly as high as 18,000 feet.

#704 The bumblebee bat, or Kitti's hog-nosed bat, is the smallest bat species and perhaps the world's smallest mammal. They are just over an inch long and weigh less than 1/10 of an ounce. They live in limestone caves in western Thailand and southeast Burma (Myanmar).

#705 Though not 100% accurate, chickens with white ear lobes generally lay white eggs, those with red lobes lay brown eggs, and those with blue lobes lay blue eggs. Occasionally, you will see a chicken with green or iridescent lobes that will lay green eggs. There is little difference in nutritional value between the eggs.

#706 The "Unicorn of the Sea" is a narwhal whale that lives in Arctic waters. They have a single, spiral tusk that is actually a canine tooth that protrudes from the left side of the upper jaw and reaches 5-10 feet in length. Tusks from the Norwegian narwhal were used to make Denmark's Coronation Chair in the late 1600s for King Frederick III.

#707 Snake Island is a 100-acre island about 20 miles off the southeastern coast of Brazil, home to the highly venomous pit viper snake called the Golden Lancehead. The island is off-limits to the public. Between 2,000 and 4,000 of the species live on the island and are listed as critically endangered. Generally, victims bitten by the Golden Lancehead die within an hour after being bitten. Because the Golden Lancehead can bring up to $30,000 on the black market, wildlife smugglers will occasionally sneak onto the island to catch some.

More than Trivia   *Interesting Stories and Fascinating Facts*

Plants & Animals

#708 Murmuration is the flocking and swarming behavior of the starling bird when hundreds or thousands of them move together in flight, twisting and changing direction in unison at a moment's notice. Scientists are unsure how the birds coordinate their movements. Still, it is like watching the performance of an elaborate marching band in the sky.

#709 In October 1963, Felicette, a black and white stray cat, was successfully launched into space as part of the French space program. She was one of 14 cats trained for spaceflight and was named after the cartoon character Felix the Cat. Felicette has since been honored on postage stamps worldwide, and her statue is at the International Space University.

#710 Some birds are toxic to touch or eat. They do not produce or inject venom, but their body absorbs toxin from insects and plants in their diet. They can then secrete this toxin into their skin and feathers to defend themselves from predators. These birds include the pitohui and ifrita birds from New Guinea, the red warbler from Mexico, the spur-winged goose from Africa, and others.

#711 Honey made by bees can remain fresh for centuries primarily because of its low water content but also because of its acidity. Although the nectar gathered by bees has a high water content of about 70%, digestion and regurgitation between forager bees and hive bees, followed by evaporation, reduces the water content to as low as 17%. The evaporation process in a honey bee colony is quite impressive. Bees generate a lot of body heat, maintaining a temperature of around 95 degrees in the honey storage area. They use this heat and wing movement to create the ideal conditions for water evaporation, resulting in a high-quality honey product.

Interesting Stories and Fascinating Facts   **More** than Trivia

Plants & Animals

#712 A frog's tongue can snatch prey 5 times faster than you can blink. Though the tongue is covered with a saliva-like substance, the saliva becomes thicker than honey outside the mouth, sticking to its prey as it pulls it into its mouth.

#713 The Australian Christmas tree is a parasitic plant from the mistletoe family. It grows in western Australia, reaches over 30 feet tall, and produces yellow-orange flowers during the Christmas season. Locally it is known as Moodjar, and the scientific name is *Nuytsia floribunda*.

#714 The volcano rabbit is the world's second smallest rabbit weighing up to about 1.3 pounds. They live in the mountains of central Mexico and are native to four volcanoes near Mexico City. Unlike many rabbits that warn of danger by thumping their feet on the ground, the volcano rabbit emits very high-pitched sounds.

#715 There is a rare hybrid bear called a "Pizzly Bear" or "Grolar Bear." It is a cross between a Polar Bear and a Grizzly Bear, with eight confirmed cases. The naming convention for this hybrid is to use the male bear's species as the first part of the name and the female bear's species as the second part. If the father is a Polar Bear, it is called a "Pizzly Bear." If the father is a Grizzly Bear, it is called a "Grolar Bear."

#716 The Mongoose and the cobra (or any poisonous snake) are natural enemies. They each know if they don't kill their foe, their foe will probably kill them. They do not coexist. The Mongoose will win a fight against a cobra about 80% of the time. The Mongoose is very quick, but most importantly, its system is resistant (but not immune) to snake venom. They can withstand a certain amount of venom, but if they get bit often enough, they will die.

More than Trivia   *Interesting Stories and Fascinating Facts*

Plants & Animals

#717 There are 60 species of birds that do not have the ability to fly, and the penguin is perhaps the most famous among them. The largest group of these flightless birds are called ratites, and they include the ostrich, emu, and kiwi.

#718 Flamingos are not naturally pink at birth. Due to the beta-carotene in their diet, they are born with a grayish-red plumage but develop into the light pink to bright red birds we are familiar with. A well-fed, healthy flamingo is more vibrantly colored. Why flamingos usually stand on one leg with the other tucked beneath their body is unknown. Flamingos can fly, so those in captivity often require their wings to be clipped.

#719 Giant Pandas are native to China. They were only found outside China before 1984 because of a policy called Panda Diplomacy where China would give Pandas to other nations as gifts. Since 1984 however, China only offers pandas to other nations on 10-year loans. The fee for this loan is $1,000,000 a year, and any panda cubs born during the loan are the property of China. Essentially, China owns all the giant pandas in the world.

#720 Ben Franklin had a higher opinion of the wild turkey than the bald eagle, our national bird. He said the turkey was "a much more respectable bird" and "a bird of courage." Franklin said of the bald eagle, "He is a bird of bad moral character. He does not get his living honestly." He may have said this because the bald eagle will steal food from another bird in flight or from animals on the ground, especially during winter. The bald eagle is not really bald. Its name came from the Middle English word *balde*, meaning white, referring to its white head and tail feathers and their contrast with the darker body.

Plants & Animals

#721 Even monkeys floss their teeth. A Japanese macaque has been observed in the wild and captivity, flossing with human hair and feathers.

#722 Plants only use about 3% of the water they absorb from the soil, and the rest is released into the air through their leaves, stems, and flowers in a process called transpiration. When corn does this, it is called "corn sweat." An acre of corn can sweat/release up to 4,000 gallons of water vapor into the air daily.

#723 A caterpillar has no bones in its body, but it does have 4,000 muscles. The human body only has 629 muscles. Caterpillars have 12 eyes arranged in a semi-circle. Still, they have poor vision and cannot see images or colors. Caterpillars eat so much food they may end up being 100 times larger than they were when first hatched.

#724 All parts of the milkweed plant are poisonous to humans and animals. But as a caterpillar, the monarch butterfly depends on the milkweed plant leaves as its only food source. Its toxic sap does not harm them but helps protect them from predators and remains with them even after metamorphosis. As a butterfly, the Monarch feeds on the flowers of the milkweed and other plants.

#725 The Corpse Flower, (*Rafflesia arnoldii*), is a flowering plant that produces the world's largest bloom. This rare flower is found in the rainforests of Indonesia. It can grow 3 feet across and weigh up to 15 pounds. It is a parasitic plant with no visible leaves, roots, or stems. It attaches itself to a host plant to obtain water and nutrients. When in bloom, the Corpse Flower emits a repulsive odor similar to rotting meat. This odor attracts insects that pollinate the plant.

More than **Trivia** *Interesting Stories and Fascinating Facts*

Plants & Animals

#726 About one-third of all domestic cats are unaffected by catnip. The euphoric response that most cats display to catnip is hereditary.

#727 The boomslang is a highly venomous African snake. Its venom is slow-acting, and it may take hours before symptoms appear. Because of this, people that are bit sometimes think no venom was injected. Its venom is primarily a hemotoxin, and the victim may die of internal and external bleeding.

#728 The kakapo parrot of New Zealand is the only parrot of 400 species worldwide that cannot fly. The kakapo is a critically endangered species, and its total adult population is known to be 248 birds, all tagged. They live on four islands off the coast of New Zealand that have been cleared of predators. The kakapo can live to be 100 years old.

#729 The dragon tree (*Dracaena draco*) is a subtropical tree native to the Canary Islands and nearby areas. A reddish resin called dragon's blood is released when the bark or leaves are cut. Dragon's blood from the dragon tree and other related species has been used as a dye, medicine, and a source of varnish for 18th-century Italian violinmakers.

#730 Clams and mussels are mollusk types that are very good at detecting and filtering pollutants in water. They can filter up to two gallons of water per day. Warsaw Waterworks in Poland uses eight clams with sensors attached to their shells to monitor the water quality for 8 million people. If they detect polluted water, they close their shells, which sets off an alarm. The city of Minneapolis has a similar setup using 12 mussels to detect and filter water pollutants.

Interesting Stories and Fascinating Facts   **More** than **Trivia**

Plants & Animals

#731 The brown thrasher has the most extensive song repertoire of birds, having over 1,000 song types.

#732 The sound of some katydids depends on the temperature, and you can get a reasonably accurate reading this way. Generally, the number of chirps in 15 seconds plus 37 is the temperature in Fahrenheit.

#733 Lobsters have an excellent sense of smell due to four small antennae on the front of their heads and tiny sensing hairs covering their bodies. Lobsters have teeth, but they are in their stomach. The stomach is located a very short distance from the mouth, and the food is chewed between three grinding surfaces that look like molar surfaces, called the gastric mill.

#734 Those cute little energetic four-legged puff balls called French Poodles are not a dog breed. Poodles are categorized into three types according to their size - Standard, Miniature, and Toy Poodle - none of them are French Poodle. Most believe the Poodle originated in Germany instead of France, and the German word for Poodle is *Pudel*. The Poodle was originally bred for hunting and is an excellent water retriever of waterfowl and ducks.

#735 Scientists have discovered a species of palm called *Pinanga subterranea* that is somehow pollinated and develops its flowers and fruits underground. Pollination of most plants typically occurs above ground, mainly by bees and butterflies. This rare phenomenon has only been observed by an orchid named *Rhizanthella* (underground orchid). This newly discovered palm (by scientists) is native to the tropical island of Borneo in Southeast Asia, and its fruit is well known by the locals for its sweet and juicy taste.

More than Trivia   *Interesting Stories and Fascinating Facts*

Plants & Animals

#736 An owl's eyes are fixed in place, looking straight ahead. But they can rotate their head three-quarters of a full circle (270 degrees) in either direction, plus 90 degrees up and down.

#737 The TomTato is a plant that grows cherry tomatoes above ground and potatoes below ground on the same plant. Dutch company Beekenkamp Plants developed the TomTato and brought it to market in 2015.

#738 Japan gave 3,000 cherry trees to Washington, DC, in 1912 to celebrate the friendship between the U.S. and Japan. The National Cherry Blossom Festival marks the start of spring in our nation's capital and draws millions to the city every year.

#739 The Greenland shark, found in the North Atlantic and Arctic oceans, can live 400 years or longer. Its meat is toxic, but after a fermentation process of four to five months to reduce toxins, it is considered a delicacy called *hakarl* in Iceland. It has a strong ammonia smell and a fishy taste and is not for the faint of heart.

#740 Some animals, such as dogs, cats, deep-sea animals, and others, have a layer of tissue in their eye called *tapetum lucidum* that enables them to see better in the dark. This tissue is also why their pupil appears to glow, an effect called eyeshine. Green eyeshine occurs in cats, dogs, and raccoons. Red eyeshine occurs in coyotes, rodents, opossums, and birds, and blue eyeshine occurs in horses.

Interesting Stories and Fascinating Facts **More** than **Trivia**

Chapter 20

Geography

#741 Dotsero is an active volcano located in western Colorado, about 5 miles from Utah, near the convergence of the Colorado and Eagle Rivers. Its last eruption occurred around 4,200 years ago during the time that the Egyptian pyramids were being built. The U.S. Geological Survey classifies it as a moderately dangerous volcano, and there is a mobile home park at the base of the volcano.

#742 Mount Everest, the highest mountain in the world and located in the Himalayan Mountain Range, was named after British surveyor Sir George Everest. He never saw the mountain and objected to it being named after him. Sir George hired Andrew Scott Waugh, who made the first formal observations of the peak. Waugh recommended it be named after Everest. There were several local native names for the mountain, which translated to Holy Mother, Holy Mountain, or Goddess of the Sky. The British initially called it "Peak b" and later "Peak XV." Despite Sir George's objections, the Royal Geographic Society named the peak after him in 1865, one year before his death.

Interesting Stories and Fascinating Facts   **More** than *Trivia*

Geography

#743 Africa is the only continent with land in all four hemispheres (Northern, Southern, Eastern, and Western). The equator divides the earth into northern and southern hemispheres. In contrast, the Prime Meridan, where longitude is defined as 0 degrees, divides the globe into the eastern and western hemispheres.

#744 Lake Hillier, in Western Australia, has high salt content levels, much like the Dead Sea. But what is unusual about Lake Hillier is its vibrant pink color caused by the lake's red algae and red bacteria. Despite the high salt content, the lake is safe to swim in and has no adverse effects on people. The pink color is permanent and does not change when put into a container.

#745 Though it's only 9 inches in diameter, the Kola Superdeep Borehole on the Kola Peninsula near the Russian border with Norway is over 7.6 miles deep and is the deepest borehole in the world. Though they wanted to drill deeper, the project was stopped in 1994 due to insufficient funds. Because of higher-than-expected temperatures at that depth, drilling deeper was considered unfeasible. Exploring this deep frontier has many scientific benefits but is challenging and expensive.

#746 Lake Superior, located on the border of Canada and the United States, is the world's largest freshwater lake by surface area. It spans 350 miles in length and holds 2,900 cubic miles of water. With over 200 rivers flowing into it, the lake contains 10% of the world's fresh water. In 2019, the Coast Guard put the Superior Entry Lighthouse (Wisconsin Point Lighthouse) on Lake Superior up for sale. Steven Broudy, a San Francisco tech company VP and former Army Ranger, purchased the century-old lighthouse for $159,000 sight unseen. His goal is to restore the lighthouse to its original glory.

More than Trivia *Interesting Stories and Fascinating Facts*

Geography

#747 The ground under the city of Amsterdam is soft clay, and buildings would sink into the ground if they used standard building techniques. Amsterdam's buildings sit upon about 11 million long wooden poles sunk into the ground 35 feet to 60 feet deep.

#748 The largest unclaimed territory on Earth is called Marie Byrd Land. It is an unclaimed region of Antarctica comprising 620,000 square miles. It was named after the wife of American naval officer Richard E. Byrd, who explored the area in the early 20th century.

#749 Did you ever wonder why several countries (Afghanistan, Kazakhstan, Kyrgyzstan, Tajikistan, Pakistan, Turkmenistan, and Uzbekistan) in Central Asia end with "stan?" It's not because Laurel (Stan) and Hardy were popular there. It is because *stan* is a Persian word for "country" or "place of."

#750 The world's tallest uninterrupted waterfall is Angel Falls in Venezuela. It has a height of over 3,200 feet and a plunge of over 2,600 feet. The falls are named after a U.S. aviator, Jimmie Angel, who was the first person to fly over the falls. When Angel died in 1960, his ashes were scattered over the falls.

#751 Zealandia is a mostly submerged continent in the South Pacific that is almost the size of Australia. New Zealand is part of this submerged continent that rises above the sea, as is New Caledonia. Zealandia was noticed for the first time by American geophysicist Bruce Luyendyk in 1995. Satellite measurements made in 2002 showed the rough outline of the submerged continent, which was confirmed later and made public in 2017.

Interesting Stories and Fascinating Facts   **More** than **Trivia**

Geography

#752 Even though Australia has almost 150 volcanoes, none are active, and it is the only continent without any active volcanoes.

#753 Maine is the closest U.S. state to Africa. Quoddy Head Light, Maine, is 3,331.8 miles from Morocco, Africa, while the assumed closest state of Florida is 4,084.9 miles away.

#754 There are over half a million acres of uninhabited land called Bir Tawil along the border between Egypt and Sudan, which neither country claims. It has a hot desert climate and is 120 miles from the Red Sea. Because it is an unclaimed territory, several individuals and organizations have tried to claim it as a micronation, but they have yet to be recognized by any government.

#755 The Great Barrier Reef is the world's largest coral reef system, comprising over 2,900 individual reefs and 900 islands stretching over 400 miles. It is in the Coral Sea, off the coast of Queensland, Australia, and can be seen from outer space. It is the world's biggest single structure made by living organisms. It is composed of and built by billions of tiny organisms known as coral polyps.

More than **Trivia**   *Interesting Stories and Fascinating Facts*

Chapter 21

Weather & Astronomy

#756 Lightning can sometimes seem to strike out of a clear blue sky. This occurs when lightning emerges from the side of a thunderstorm cloud and travels horizontally for several miles before descending vertically to strike the ground. This type of lightning is sometimes called anvil lightning, and can travel as far as 10 miles from its originating thunderstorm cloud.

#757 NASA launched the *Voyager 1* spacecraft over 45 years ago to fly by Jupiter and Saturn to collect data. It passed that landmark, crossed into interstellar space (no longer affected by our sun) in August 2012, and continues collecting data. *Voyager 1* carries two phonograph records called the Voyager Golden Records with various sounds and images for anyone who may find them. A committee chaired by Carl Sagan selected the record contents. The music includes classical, blues, and Chuck Berry's rock and roll song "Johnny B. Goode." Sagan wanted to include the Beatle's song "Here Comes the Sun," but the record company that held the copyrights declined.

Weather & Astronomy

#758 "Once in a blue moon" is an expression that means not very often. Blue moon most often refers to an extra full moon that occurs in a yearly cycle. There are typically three full moons in winter, spring, summer, and fall, for 12 in an annual cycle. But every once in a while, a year contains 13 full moons, and the extra one is called a blue moon. Even rarer is when the moon appears blue because of certain atmospheric conditions, such as a volcano eruption.

#759 In August 2006, the International Astronomical Union (IAU) downgraded the status of Pluto from a full-sized planet to that of a dwarf planet because it did not meet all three criteria it developed for a full-sized planet. This was an unpopular decision in many circles. The New Mexico House of Representatives passed a resolution in honor of Clyde Tombaugh, the discoverer of Pluto and a longtime resident of that state, that declared that Pluto will always be considered a planet while in New Mexican skies and that March 13, 2007, was Pluto Planet Day.

#760 The Leonid meteor shower occurs yearly like clockwork in mid-November, typically with 10-15 meteors per hour. The Leonid meteors are made from the debris of the comet Tempel-Tuttle and are some of the longest-lasting meteors to see. Tempel-Tuttle completes an orbit around the sun about every 33 years, releasing new debris at that time. A meteor shower becomes a meteor storm when it produces over 1,000 meteors per hour. Hundreds of thousands of meteors were seen during the Leonid meteor storm of 1833. Another spectacular meteor storm in 1966 produced 2,000-3,000 meteors per minute for a brief time. An episode of the TV show *Malcolm in the Middle* in 2000 revolves around an attempt to view the Leonid meteors.

More than Trivia *Interesting Stories and Fascinating Facts*

Weather & Astronomy

#761 Because thunder is a sound wave, it makes different sounds depending on its proximity, air temperature, and type of lightning strike. A crack or bang of thunder indicates a nearby thunderstorm with a lightning bolt most likely striking the ground, and a rumble of thunder suggests a more distant storm.

#762 Watching clouds float across the sky, we may think they are almost weightless. However, a single cumulus cloud can weigh over 1 million pounds because of all the water it contains. Clouds float because the density of the cloud is less than the dry air beneath it. That is the same reason oil floats on water; it is less dense than water.

#763 In December 2018, a meteor weighing 1,500 tons and measuring 32 feet across exploded in the earth's atmosphere with the force of 10 atomic bombs. The meteor was largely undetected because it was relatively small for a meteor, and it shattered over the Bering Sea between Russia and Alaska, miles from inhabited land. Missile monitoring satellites detected the blast and gave scientists enough data for basic information about the meteor.

#764 Venetia Burney is credited with naming the planet Pluto in 1930 when she was 11 after her grandfather mentioned the discovery of the new planet he had read about in a newspaper. Through an unlikely series of events, the name suggestion made its way to the Lowell Observatory in Arizona, where astronomer Clyde Tombaugh, who discovered Pluto, worked. He liked the name because it started with the initials of Percival Lowell, the observatory's founder, where the discovery was made. When Pluto was publicly announced to be the new planet's name, Venetia's grandfather rewarded her with a five-pound note.

Interesting Stories and Fascinating Facts **More** than **Trivia**

Weather & Astronomy

#765 On July 27, 1943, flying a single-engine AT6, Lieutenant Ralph O'Hair and Colonel Buckworth were the first to fly into a hurricane. It started regular Air Force flights into hurricanes.

#766 In August 1977, a radio signal from outer space lasting 72 seconds was detected by a radio telescope at Ohio State searching for extraterrestrial intelligence. The signal's origin, coming from the constellation Sagittarius, was dubbed the "Wow! Signal" and has remained a mystery for over 40 years. In 2017, a theory was proposed that the signal was a natural phenomenon caused by two comets in the area at the time. In 2020, another theory said it came from a system with a sun-like star similar to ours 1,800 light-years away in the constellation Sagittarius. No one knows where the signal came from or what it says. It may be aliens trying to find life in the universe, or perhaps an E.T. somewhere dialed the wrong number when ordering alien pizza.

#767 Tropical storms and hurricanes are named because it is an easier way to identify and remember them than any other method. Five storm/cyclone organizations worldwide create name lists for storms in their area. They each have their own naming rules and procedures, but they are similar and use names familiar to the people in their region. For example, the region that includes the Caribbean, the Gulf of Mexico, and the North Atlantic area uses six lists in rotation (the 2022 list will be reused in 2028). The list of names covers 21 of the 26 letters of the alphabet (Q, U, X, Y, and Z are not used), and the list alternates between male and female names. The year's first storm begins with an "A," the second with a "B," and so on. A supplemental name list is used if the number of storms in a year exceed 21. The list uses English, French, and Spanish names to reflect the geographical coverage, and a name will be retired from future use if it is a particularly damaging storm

More than Trivia   *Interesting Stories and Fascinating Facts*

Weather & Astronomy

#768 Sunny day rain is called a sun shower in the U.S. In Korea, one term for it is fox rain, referring to a legend about a tiger marrying a fox, causing a cloud, who loved the fox, to weep behind the sun.

#769 A rainbow is not something that can be physically approached. It is an optical illusion caused by water droplets viewed from a particular angle relative to a light source. Even if you see someone that appears to be at the end of a rainbow, they cannot see that.

#770 Lightning causes thunder. The energy from a lightning bolt heats the surrounding air to above 50,000 degrees Fahrenheit in a few millionths of a second. As this pressurized air expands, it creates a shock wave for about 30 feet, after which it becomes a sound wave or thunder.

#771 That earthy scent you smell after rainfall is called petrichor. When raindrops land on a porous surface like soil, air from the pores in the soil forms small bubbles. These bubbles float to the surface and release aerosols that carry the ground's odor into the air. Petrichor is more apparent after a light rain than a heavy one. Camels use petrichor to find water sources in the desert.

#772 The high winds in southern Colorado in mid-October 2022 created an odd, creepy experience for one Fountain, Colorado, couple. The winds caused tumbleweeds to blow against their house up to the windows, blocking the front door, surrounding their car, and blocking access to the road. Neighbors helped them mow enough of the tumbleweeds to clear a path from their driveway to the street, but they had to hire a landscaper to remove the rest of them.

Interesting Stories and Fascinating Facts **More** than **Trivia**

Weather & Astronomy

#773 Only four states had no earthquakes between 1975 and 1995 – Florida, Iowa, North Dakota, and Wisconsin. Currently, Florida and North Dakota have the smallest number of earthquakes.

#774 There is a phenomenon called a moonbow similar to a sunlight rainbow. Moonbows are very faint and usually appear to the eyes to be white. However, the colors of the moonbow can be seen in long-exposure photographs.

#775 Thundersnow is when lightning and thunder occur in a snowstorm rather than a thunderstorm. It is not very common and typically occurs above the surface where the temperatures are warmer. The lightning that happens in thundersnow can sometimes appear pink or green.

#776 Hail is the solid ice that forms inside thunderstorm updrafts. Hailstorms occur most frequently in Nebraska, Colorado, and Wyoming. The area where those three states meet is called Hail Alley. However, the largest hailstone ever recovered in the U.S. was in Vivian, South Dakota, on June 23, 2010. It weighed 1 lb. 15 oz. and was 8 inches across.

#777 From 1992-2021, the United States averaged 1,232 tornadoes each year. The states with the most tornadoes per year are Texas (139), Kansas (84), Oklahoma (66), Florida (57), Illinois (54), Iowa (51), and Nebraska (50). The states with the least tornadoes are Alaska, Hawaii, Rhode Island with 0, Delaware, New Hampshire, Vermont with 1, and Connecticut, Massachusetts, Maine, Nevada, Utah, and West Virginia with 2. Most tornadoes occur in April, May, and June.

More than Trivia *Interesting Stories and Fascinating Facts*

Other books by B. Craig Jones

Slow Down Turtle is a story about a turtle who did not realize how special he was. Rather than embracing his own uniqueness, he wanted to be like his friends. But through a series of adventures, he discovered just how special he really was.

A book of original "Nonsense Rhymes" that children will love to hear and read. Edward Lear and Lewis Carroll popularized this style in the 19th century, and others have continued it up to the present day. *Silly Rhymes for Boys & Girls* is sure to get a giggle out of the young ones and those that are young at heart.

Gratitude is part of a healthy lifestyle. It's good for us mentally, emotionally, and physically. There is so much to be grateful for regardless of all the negativity in the world. This book can help bring those things to mind by listing 777 of the more memorable or common reasons to be grateful. You can develop a good sense and practice of gratitude and reap the benefits that go with it.

This year-long journal allows you to write things you are grateful for and things you did well each day. Spending just a few minutes each day to do this can produce meaningful results in your life. The path of your life may seem unencumbered, or it may have thorns and complications. In either case, I urge you to use this simple journal to help you travel the path you are on. It could make all the difference.